T0167910

PENGUIN BOOKS

THERE ARE ~~NO~~ FALLING STARS IN CHINA

Marga Ortigas is a seasoned international correspondent and the author of *The House on Calle Sombra*, published by PRH SEA in 2021. Before turning her hand to fiction, she travelled the world for nearly three decades as a journalist, with a career spanning five continents and two of the largest global news networks. She got her start on Philippine TV, then joined CNN in London, working across Europe and covering the Iraq War from its inception. In 2006, she returned to Manila and the Asia Pacific region, reporting from the frontlines of armed conflict and climate change as senior correspondent for Al Jazeera. Her extensive coverage of the Muslim rebellion in the southern Philippines was recognized by the International Committee of the Red Cross for Humanitarian Reporting.

A British Council Chevening Scholar, Ortigas earned her MA in literature and criticism at the University of Greenwich. She speaks three languages, and is the editor of *I, Migrant*, an online platform which showcases writing from the diaspora, advocating a universal humanity beneath people's differences.

She is on social media as @margaortigas.

Also by Marga Ortigas

The House on Calle Sombra, Penguin Random House SEA, 2021

There Are ~~No~~ Falling Stars In China

& Other Life Lessons From a Recovering Journalist

Marga Ortigas

PENGUIN BOOKS

An imprint of Penguin Random House

PENGUIN BOOKS

USA | Canada | UK | Ireland | Australia
New Zealand | India | South Africa | China | Southeast Asia

Penguin Books is part of the Penguin Random House group of companies
whose addresses can be found at global.penguinrandomhouse.com

Published by Penguin Random House SEA Pte Ltd
9, Changi South Street 3, Level 08-01,
Singapore 486361

First published in Penguin Books by Penguin Random House SEA 2023

Copyright © Marga Ortigas 2023

ISBN 9789815127898

Typeset in Garamond by MAP Systems, Bengaluru, India

www.penguin.sg

For Katherine.
To the power of dreams
and silver linings.

'Silence is the language of God, all else is poor translation.'
—Jalaluddin Rumi, thirteenth-century Sufi poet

Contents

PROLOGUE

THE BIT BEFORE WE GET ON WITH IT.

Memory is a funny thing.

We commit events, people, places, emotions, smells, tastes, and all other manner of sensation to some ethereal, intangible space within which we can then only re-grasp through words. Without words, there is only the abstract. The feeling. The sensation. Sometimes that is enough.

But when we share stories of the past, as humans are wont to do, they must be articulated. And that act of conveyance—of putting those memories into form or re-collecting for the purpose of expression—inevitably alters the reality. Whether we're aware of it or not.

Because words change things. As do emotions.

Storytellers—including journalists and those we interview—put things into words *after*. That's when we try to make sense of what's been experienced when we attempt to organize thoughts and feelings. After the event. After the disaster. After the heartbreak.

After the fact.

At least, in my experience.

Once Upon a Time

In one way or another, I've been telling stories most of my life. For more than twenty-five years, it was as a journalist. Travelling across continents and meeting countless people, often in the most difficult and extraordinary of circumstances. It was work—but by golly, I *loved* it. We were on call 24/7 and there was no escape, but that was part of the job and I was always ready to jump. I never missed a deadline and had suitcases prepared according to potential assignments:

a) natural calamities—solid-coloured rain gear, mosquito repellent, and trekking shoes,

b) political and economic debacles—solid-coloured dress shirts, a suit jacket, and comfortable boots,

c) and areas of conflict—all the above, protective hardware, and then some.

There were times I would wake up in one country and get to bed in another, not knowing where I'd be the following week. Forget trying to make plans for the weekend, your phone could ring and off you'd go towards breaking news. My mother advised me to keep a diary, if only to keep track of where I was geographically. One day—she said—I'd be glad to be able to look back and see things in 'black and white'.

I wish I'd listened to my mother.

Looking back now, I find that most of what's left to me of those years is on the video clips we broadcast, which found eternal life online. Or in old photographs of strangers in now unfamiliar spaces. I look at these reminders and for a moment am transported back. To times and places I often no longer recall outside of these captured images—which can fool you into thinking that something fleeting is immortalized. It isn't. Not really. Everything changes. Like an ocean in constant flow. And memories blur together like a montage on fast-forward. Spooling itself into oblivion.

The First Frame

My earliest memory may actually be of telling myself a story. Sitting in the backseat of my father's car, stuck in unmoving city traffic. To pass the time, I'd imagine the lives of people in the other vehicles. Who they were. Where they were headed, and why. Maybe I was five or six?

A year or so later, I was drawing my own comics. Nothing fancy, just stick figures. And my characters were my neighbourhood playmates, just doing neighbourhood things. So, there was a lot of biking, visiting each other's houses, and eating. And the only reason I can tell you this now is because I found said comics.

Another memory aid recently unearthed: cassette tape recordings of my earliest narratives. It seems I progressed to crafting rather uneventful mysteries. Producing an 'audiobook' decades before Audible existed. ☺

It told of a young sleuth (maybe nine years old) finding lost historical objects. Objects—such as an 'Aztec idol'—that I knew nothing about, other than likely seeing them in some cartoon. But I mean if Nancy Drew could do it, why not my alter ego, Susan Baker? I remember choosing her name deliberately. She had to be just like those typical, clean-cut American kids we in the Philippines were inundated with on TV. I even coerced my younger sisters to act out scripts. (Indeed, do add playwright to my list of 'talents.')

But I need no memory aid for my obsession with showtunes. My mother—who taught literature and was always surrounded by books—starred in many local productions of musicals before she married. Music was constantly played at home, and my siblings and I were hooked on soundtracks before even seeing a show. Of course, this prompted me to also write a musical. (Don't ask! My younger sisters still make fun of it.)

Bottomline: It was a house and a childhood filled with stories ... and storytelling in its many forms. Offering a wondrous approach to processing—and expanding—the world.

Now here's the story of a moment that I don't recall. It was a Sunday. We were in Church. I was around two. My mother said that I was quiet until I spotted a man in the next pew who had no arms. Apparently, I then peppered my father with questions. Flummoxed, he told me to ask my mom. She tried to get me to focus on the priest, but I put my tiny hands on either side of her face and drew her to me. To her embarrassment, I asked, at the top of my two-year-old lungs: 'Why does that man have no arms?'

In a hush, she replied, 'Because God made him that way.' Thinking that would end the conversation.

She told me I tapped her arm again and asked: 'Why him, and not me?'

At that, my mother said she failed to reply.

I'll bet my two-year-old self came up with a story to fill the gap in comprehension. And I know I am not alone in such an exercise. We all do it. Even if just for personal consumption. We all tell ourselves stories and form our own narratives to explain the world.

For me, it seemed inevitable that I'd become a reporter. Asking questions, pursuing answers, seeking comprehension. Examining our larger human neighbourhood.

Which brings me back to my original question: When all is said—and sung—and done, what do we hold on to in a lifetime? Why do we recall certain things and not others? And if we don't *remember*, what then keeps things real? What is it that ultimately matters?

With time, the illusion of memory gets even more distant. Is something still of consequence if we forget?

Smoke and Mirrors

To try and grasp things or nail them down, we impotently use words. An inadequate sequence of letters from the alphabet. An attempt to encapsulate fading images in transmutable language. It's like endeavouring to pin down a fish in a river.

Often what we 'remember' is only as clear as the words used to capture it. Illusory and fragile. Like a spider's web. Or smog. A deceptively thin veil of grey molecules that can suffocate, one particle at a time.

Such is memory. An analogue[1] signal that, unlike digital codes, varies and distorts with time.

So, in this current high-tech digital world of instantaneous images, what analogue transmission do I have to share with you? And why oh why would it even matter?

Do I tell you about witnessed world events that directed the course of humanity? Expose secrets that can bring down a government or destroy careers? Or should I write about the death of my parents, each of whom passed away quietly when there was an environmental disaster at their doorstep affecting thousands of people?

Perhaps I should expound on what world leaders and corrupt politicians were really like when the cameras weren't rolling.

---

1 For Millennials and generations thereafter: Before the digital technology that powers mobile phones, laptops, and smart devices, information was transmitted through electric pulses of varying amplitude. Yes, it was as archaic and mysterious as it sounds. To learn more, do a search on your smartphone!

Maybe I can tell you which celebrities made reporters cry and how much money exchanged hands to keep potential scandals from being broadcast.

Or do I share with you how cleaning out my parents' home after they died taught me more about life than any amount of time in a warzone?

Pinpricks

In twenty-five years, there were global health crises and economic downturns, super typhoons and earthquakes, armed conflicts, human cruelty, and nuclear accidents. Caught up in all that, there was Lola Pilar. And Rupert Macawili. 'Kamikaze Sato' and Yukimitsu Saitu. The Miparanum brothers. Clarita Ala. 'Jesse'. And 'Boy'. Mama Kong. Norman Surplus. Charles and Marla. Yasser.

Janice Joy Pampangan.

And Duraid.

Just a few of the cosmic threads that pulled at me, leaving indelible marks.

And so, this 'analogue' collection. Because there is yet no technological advancement to instantaneously communicate heart. That which is at the core of our human experience. That which gives it meaning.

After twenty-five years, here I am still finding the sense of poetry in everything. Expecting to constantly discover the gentle beauty in the difficult to comprehend, and attempting to put it all in a neat, pretty, little box. Like a haiku or a song. A peek into life's infinite mysteries in three lines or three minutes.

Like a TV news report.

Except on television, we were allotted even less time. Two minutes, at most. To try and capture 'real life' as it unfolded. In snippets. Images. Faces. Words. Montage on montage. A pastiche that played itself out until you no longer saw the individual frames.

The 'news'. In the age of twenty-four-hour media, it's become reality on steroids. Hyper-truth. Whirling itself out of control.

So, now—'*fake news?*' ~~Altered realism~~.

What is truth if we cannot hold on to it? ~~Analogue~~.

'Post-Reality'

Describing myself as a journalist doesn't give what I've put down here any more weight. I am but a storyteller. As we all are. Passing time, sharing experiences, trying to understand.

We are all magicians. Artists. Reflectors of light. Holding mirrors up to each other. That should carry weight enough of its own.

I am a storyteller. Making a futile attempt to capture the uncapturable.

In more than twenty-five years, I've seen quite a bit on assignment for international news networks—but so have we all, thanks to the wonders of digital media. At the flick of a screen, the immediacy of war. Disease. Suffering. Even triumph and joy. There are tons of material for a more *serious* book examining the intricacies of geopolitics, social trends, what-not—and many such variations have already been written. This is not one of them.

These are just some of the stories I **remember**, the little joys or woes off-camera that have stayed with me. And I share them in the hope that they might strike a chord—and that you find a bit of yourself in them, too. Because like you, journalists are but storytellers. And reality is a funny, analogue thing.

Do forgive my poor translation.

THE PHILIPPINES

By the River Pasig

Manila

SOMETIMES, THE BEHOLDER'S EYES ARE CROSSED.

I will start at the beginning—and the beginning will always be Manila.

Home

We have a very chequered relationship, the crowded, chaotic, cacophonous megapolis and me. Not uncommon, I would think, between people and the places they grew up in.

When I think of Manila, I see a massive black hole of tangled frenzy. Like an excessively energetic giant atom. Oppressively dynamic.

For me, it was instinctive. Barely five years old, still oblivious to the city's challenging social realities, and yet, already dreaming of escape. Seriously. My most vivid childhood dreams were of flight. Of leaving the place of my birth, where the quotidian tediousness was stifling me before I could even understand why.

The desire to flee was so strong that it stretched my imagination to the point of frightening my playmates. Many of whom did not seem to enjoy the games of aliens and other inter-planetary travellers that I came up with for us to play.

3

When I couldn't coerce anyone into a round of these space adventures, I pretended I was not human. That I was sent to Earth on a mission to study its inhabitants and report regularly back to my 'boss' on another planet.

Don't get me wrong—I was not some exceedingly curious wonderkid. It was not about a need to *explore* as much as a desire to *be* from someplace else. Somewhere, clearly, far, far away. I honestly have no explanation for it. It's not like I grew up in an unhappy home.

Rome

When I was eight, I asked my parents to take me to Rome. Completely oblivious to the fact that such a trip would be difficult and costly. You see, I had to do a school report on the Italian capital and fell in love. It seemed such an extraordinary place. The Colosseum, the Vatican (which I do realize is its own entity), the Pantheon, the Tiber River, the Trevi Fountain, Castel Sant'Angelo—and pasta! Determined little me was fixated on getting there someday. So, I made a wish and tucked it away in my little alien heart.

A decade later, an opportunity arose to visit Europe with a group of similarly aged teens, and I finally made it to Rome thanks to a summer job that came out of nowhere (serendipity) and provided the funds. (A whole other story.)

That was my first 'solo' trip out of the Philippines, and I was so clueless about travel that I packed a rucksack full of snacks for the flight. M&Ms, cups of yogurt, packets of crisps, and boxes of chocolate. Unaware that, of course, the airline would feed you on the plane! (I ate my own snacks, too, anyway.)

Flight

But before that trip, all through my childhood I dreamt of flying across the skies, high above reality. Not that I wanted to be superwoman or anything like that. I didn't fantasize about having a red cape or the strength of steel. I just wanted to fly. A plane of my own would do. Or a giant balloon. A magic carpet or a kite. Even teleportation. All of these 'methods' inhabited my dreams. More specifically, I dreamt about dreaming it. That is: I dreamt of flight—but never actually *flew* anywhere in my sleep.

Many of these dreams had me sitting on a plane with the seatbelt fastened, excitement bubbling—but I would always wake up before take-off.

Once, I was in a majestic hot air balloon. It seemed so real I could feel the basket underneath me and the ropes that fastened it to the balloon. Finally, I was in flight! I could feel the wind in my face and the change in the atmosphere as I went from one part of the globe to another. The heat of the deserts, the chill of the Arctic, the afternoon's soft touch over Paris. Can you imagine how thrilled I was when I spotted the Colosseum? Finally—Rome!

But just as I thought I was getting the hang of controlling the balloon, it lost air and dropped closer to the ground. Close enough for me to realize that I wasn't actually flying over the world's most magical places but was suspended in a theatrical prop held up by invisible cables over miniature models of cities. Talk about being deflated. I was but a foolish wannabe-Gulliver in a fake Lilliput.

My point though—I was born in Manila and for some reason always had a singular dream: to leave.

Plight

Please don't get me wrong. As I said earlier, by no stretch of the imagination did I have a terrible childhood that I needed to get away from. Quite the contrary. My parents were wonderful. And they kept my siblings and I housed, fed, clothed, and sent us to school. In a developing country under martial rule, with a high incidence of poverty and child employment, we knew these were luxuries not afforded to all. A childhood free of anxiety—and with time for play—was an opulence unavailable to millions.

Fright

Ultimately, the world turned out to be much uglier than I was prepared for. And it all rushed in as soon as I was no longer confined to the safe little bubble of such a childhood. The country's deep social divisions were visible not only in its unruly urban landscapes but right in people's homes, where everything—and everyone—had its place. The right environment for entitled bullies to proliferate. Worse, most others just assumed powerlessness and accepted the dysfunctional social order as a matter of course.

Outside the safe bubble, totalitarian rule was the norm—as were crime, corruption, and fear.

A memory long tucked away and only recently unpacked: I was around eight years old and starting fourth grade in a new school. Classes were suspended almost as soon as they'd begun. Why? A school security guard, whose name I distinctly remember, was hacked to death in one of the toilets after he foiled an attempted hostage-taking. This outlandish crime was obviously not discussed or explained to us students, but looking back now, it was hard not to see that life was cheap in the Philippines.

Most of us students were spared the horrific scene of that killing, but even as children, we couldn't be kept oblivious for long to what was happening. Some of us had classmates whose parents were killed in their homes by government agents or thrown in detention centres and later disappeared.

It was not uncommon for these *occurrences* to go unreported—a free press didn't really exist until the long-reigning dictator was deposed in the late 1980s. Even after that, such incidents happened so regularly, they didn't seem to qualify as news.

I was in my teens the first time I was directly exposed to a gruesome crime. A man in a T-shirt and shorts lying dead in a mall's open-air parking lot. I remember one of his flip-flops had come off his foot. He'd been shot in the head. Which was surrounded by a murky pool of blood so dark it was almost black on the pavement. That was ... quite a sight. I don't know what really happened or if the police ever came. But I can tell you this: I was old enough then to read the newspapers and there was not a word about the man in the mall parking lot who was shot in the head.

There were traffic jams caused by lifeless bodies dumped on roadsides or angry motorists brandishing guns to get right of way.

And frankly, such a dichotomy—between so-called polite society and brutal reality—was more than slightly obscene.

Maybe there was a deep, subconscious reason for my desire to flee.

Sight

I was a twenty-three-year-old journalist with five years of experience when I left Manila in the late nineties. Offered a place *abroad*—London—to study the crafted stories of other cultures.

After that, I went on to join a wee international news organization called CNN, which eventually put me back on the path from whence I came.

There's much to be said about how travel expands our perspectives and challenges our expectations.

After almost six years at CNN in London and nearly a decade away from the Philippines, a new global news channel—Al Jazeera English—laid out a world map before me and asked that I set up one of their bureaux in a location of my choice. Little did I know how tough it would be to pioneer a station that few beyond the Middle East knew about or trusted. To their surprise (and mine!), I picked Manila—which wasn't even on their list of options. I found myself eager to return to Asia and tell stories from a place then overlooked and misunderstood.

My bosses gave me two years to prove the city a worthwhile base for a bureau or I would agree to be relocated.

Nearly twenty years on and the network still has its office in Manila.

When we established the bureau in 2006, the Philippine capital was glossier than when I left. It had more skyscrapers and less green spaces, wider roads and narrower pavements. But there were also more shanties and street children. And that contradictory reality ... well, it served to reiterate that little had changed. Bullies were still in power and the powerless remained in their lane. The nation's coffers continued to be ransacked and natural calamities, like clockwork, came with a vengeance.

Basically, my job entailed watching disasters unfold and feudal/tribalistic traditions be transformed into what passed for democracy—then, explaining it all to those outside of it.

At the time, a former CNN colleague from London was travelling through Asia, and I hoped to convince him to accept the offer of a job in Al Jazeera's new Manila bureau. I let him know the office would be in the country's equivalent of Hollywood, thinking that might entice him to join me. He never let me forget that higgledy-piggledy Quezon City (QC) didn't quite match up to what he expected.

In truth, QC was where most national TV stations had their studios. It was chaotic—like when 'best laid plans' clearly go awry—scabrous, uninspiring, and noisy. Frankly, more like Hollywood than he realized.

In all the years we worked together out of that bureau, he and I crisscrossed the country witnessing calamities, corruption, and camaraderie. The resilience and the passion of Filipinos. Their acceptance of and patience with terrible governments, and their disillusion with good ones. In other words, we **paid attention**. We had to. That was the job. At every stage, we had to be **in the moment**. Open to and aware of everything going on around us, to better understand and digest. It was a vital lesson for me. To always **be present.** No matter where I was.

Perhaps at some point in our lives, we all long to flee the perceived shackles of the cultures we are born into. But by getting to bear witness to so much, I learnt that people's foibles aren't necessarily predetermined by their heritage.

We met so many amazing individuals while on assignment, each doing their best to push forward despite adversity.

Through all this—and assisted by my British colleague's fresh perspective—my love-hate relationship with Manila was tempered further. I blinked and realized that I just needed to reorient my focus.

I learnt to breathe in every second and not yearn for escape.

No More Dirigibles

I no longer dream of flight or hot air balloons.

And I now see that I'm not the only 'alien' in existence. There are many of us trying to make sense of a world that overwhelms and constantly upends our expectations.

As my colleague once put it when we were returning to Manila after an international assignment: 'It may very well be the ugliest city in the world—but it's home.'

After all the trips and a decade of being based elsewhere, this is the biggest lesson I learnt: you can't run away from your roots or what is within. There is only **adjusting your vision** and discovering that **even in chaos there is poetry**.

Sulu

SOMETIMES, THE GUIDEBOOKS ARE WRONG.

A Beautiful Minefield

Like a collection of endangered turtle eggs in deceptively opalesque waters, the Sulu Islands are among the most beautiful in the Philippines. Pearlescent white against crystal blue.

Well, *technically*, they form part of the greater, archipelagic Philippine state—but many of Sulu's inhabitants would rather they be recognized as an Islamic nation. Separate from the larger and largely Christian Philippines.

For its pristine waters, white sand beaches, thick mangroves, and lush jungles—Sulu should be in all the tourist guidebooks.

But it isn't.

It should be featured in geographic and historical journals for—among other things—the little-seen, jungle-covered stone ruins of an ancient sultanate's palace.

But it isn't.

At this writing, island officials are only just beginning to encourage visitors, welcoming tourists so long as they first register with the local government. Authorities say it's for the purposes of 'coordination', which suggests that it's for their safety. There are still headlines from Sulu about the activities of suspected terrorists. The place has a reputation for violence. Decades of armed clashes, targeted killings, and bombings.

Many indigenous Islamic tribes call it home, and besides fighting the national government for autonomy—they're known to fight amongst each other, too.

The people of Sulu will tell you that's just the way it is.

That lawlessness and instability are normal.

That along with insurgents—bandits, vigilantes, and all other gunowners rule.

This also means that progress and development haven't had a chance to roost. Leaving impoverished residents looking for any way they can to earn a living. Not an easy task in a socio-political—and sometimes literal—minefield.

For years, kidnappings-for-ransom and/or intimidation were rampant—as were assassinations-for-a-fee.

It was a hotbed of gun-running, piracy on the high seas, and armed robberies. And known to provide smugglers—of people and other commodities—with a large swathe of opportunities.

Hence, the lack (so far) of tourists to beautiful Sulu. It has spent more time on international lists of places *not* to visit.

No Man's Land

The first time I went—or rather, was *sent* there—I was petrified. It was 2006 and I was on an assignment for Al Jazeera, a brand-new international news channel. The first one to broadcast in English from a base in the Middle East. We hoped that would help locals see us as a less unpalatable entity.

Due to the aforementioned risks, few outside journalists visited Sulu to assess the situation first hand, relying instead on local stringers for information.

But it is difficult to gain a true understanding of a place unless you have walked along its pockmarked streets, smelled the mystifying allure of its undernourished markets, and shared a meal with its frightened residents. Short of that and you are cobbling together a one-dimensional facsimile. So, as terrified as I may have been, I was also glad for the chance to *experience* Sulu.

From the moment we landed at its small airport, my cameraman and I were accompanied by a security escort from the governor's office. I can't recall exactly how many men there were, but every one of them was armed to the teeth. And we couldn't make a move without them.

As you may already surmise, that same armed escort meant to keep us safe also limited our access to information. Because of their presence, we were only welcome where our host—their boss—was welcome. And in Sulu—with its numerous unmarked fiefdoms—that wasn't many places.

Sights and Savages

Much of the small archipelago was untamed—deep rain forests, mangroves, volcanoes. Yet it seemed the land had been parcelled to various factions. And without perimeter fences, it was difficult to know when one might be entering *hostile* territory.

But the locals could always tell.

You see that bridge? Don't cross it …

Stay this side of the tree. If you go past, you'll fall in trouble.

Don't walk on that beach … it's the Abu Sayyaf's …

… They're up that hillside, too.

The Abu Sayyaf. An internationally labelled terrorist group. Also known as the ASG, it began as a collective of extremist Muslims fighting for a separate state, but their political cause quickly devolved into savage banditry. They were notorious for blowing things up and beheading hostages. Then, it became all about making money.

In existence since the late 1990s, the Abu Sayyaf were woven into the fabric of modern-day Sulu like venomous termites with fangs. An infestation the locals had just got used to.

As fearful as we were to encounter the 'vermin', we risked venturing into a rainforest with some locals who wanted to show us a site previously unseen by outsiders. Security escort in tow, of course.

There, in the middle of that overrun jungle, was one of Sulu's most intriguing attractions. The ruins of what I was told was the Palace of Flowers. The seat of a once powerful sultanate that ruled a rich archipelago stretching from southern Philippines, across the Sulu Sea to modern-day Indonesia and Malaysia. All that was left of it were sections of stone—arches and walls overhung with foliage—and the last rulers' tombs speckled in moss. I know it isn't in any guidebook, and from my understanding, few others have visited.

What a waste that such poignant reminders of a rich, cultural past have remained unseen—leaving the present victim to the follies of ignorance.

I have never forgotten how surreal it was to walk among those hallowed stones. An unexpected reminder that there's always more to first impressions.

Terrorists and Teddy Bears

Speaking of first impressions …

On a later trip to Basilan, the largest of the Sulu archipelago islands, we were offered an interview with the Abu Sayyaf. What would you do in that situation? An 'exclusive' and a visit to their camp.

To be honest, such 'exclusives' were dangled before any journalist who dared set foot on their islands. And many who accepted ended up being held hostage for ransom. We had no desire to wind up a headline. So, we turned down the offer. No exclusive is worth your life.

To my surprise, two of these guys then agreed to meet us in a *neutral* location of our choice, so long as we didn't inform the authorities.

We found a place right in the middle of the town. A densely populated area. Dressed like civilians, the two ASG fighters blended in like flotsam with jetsam.

Our security stayed at a distance—trusting we were safe in a residential zone.

In a high-fenced space that was open to the elements, we sat the fighters down on wobbly plastic chairs, the only available seating we could find. They changed their clothing to conceal their identities and covered their faces with traditional black and white keffiyehs. But even disguised, there was no hiding their palpable exhaustion. Life on the run is not for the faint of heart.

As with most things in Sulu, the interview wasn't anything like we expected. Instead of fire and brimstone, the demeanour of these combatants reeked of weakness and regret. Both claimed to have only joined the group out of necessity. In a lawless place, the Abu Sayyaf was a 'gang' of sorts that gave them a sense of power. But with government forces hot on their trail, that gang was barely subsisting in the jungle and on the verge of splintering.

The men we interviewed had supposedly participated in brutal acts of decapitation that shocked the world. They were looking to reboot their lives and start afresh. The older fighter said he'd developed a conscience, while the other admitted that he was tired of being a fugitive. Both were terrified of leaving the Abu Sayyaf. Not for any legal repercussions they might face, but retaliation from their fellow vermin. That's why they hid their identities while on camera.

One combatant claimed to be a cousin of the group's most notorious leader. He was wearing a baseball cap with a logo in the shape of a target.

The other one joined the group to rebel against his parents. To prove to them, he said, that he was 'a man'. This guy was reed thin, and only bulked up by the oversized sweater he wore. In 35° C heat. The red pullover was emblazoned with a teddy bear. Not a look one might expect from the most dreaded people on the islands.

Take My Daughter

They were not the only armed fighters who surprised me.

On another island in the southern Philippines, deep in another rainforest, we encountered the same fatigue at a camp of insurgents. It was an entire village of warriors hiding in plain sight. Displaced, disgruntled families training their children to fight. A new generation of Muslim separatists.

Many of the younger folk didn't even know what they were fighting for. They were born into a war, orphaned, and handed a gun.

Among them, we met a fourteen-year-old whose gaze revealed his isolation and ignorance. When I asked him what he longed for, he automatically said he wanted peace. I asked him to expound and describe what that meant to him. His face dropped, and never once looking me in the eye, he muttered that he wasn't sure what peace was.

The children were not the only ones bearing arms. So were their mothers. We interviewed one woman who was all blazing fury and rage when the camera was rolling. Soon as we were done, she had a massive young coconut cleaved open and offered me its juice.

As I grappled to keep the giant *buko* between my hands, the woman pulled me aside to speak about her family. How they knew nothing else but poverty and war. How her husband was killed by soldiers and their children had to take up his fight. She had young boys who were training to be killers. Then, she grasped my arm and asked if I could take her daughter away from the conflict.

'Please bring her with you to Manila ... any job will do. She can cook or clean ... and wash your clothes.'

I wish I could say I suddenly acquired an assistant ... but I didn't. I did however try to find a placement for her daughter once I returned to the capital. Unfortunately, by the time I reached out with information, the woman's phone number no longer worked and I was unable to find her.

Those in Charge

Far from the large urban centres, these stunning but afflicted islands were controlled by wealthy clans who seemed to take turns enriching themselves. Vulgar bullies with their own armies, who governed as if it were a fiefdom. Some even sprung criminals out of prison to reinforce their 'staff'. How do I know this? One such convict told me himself. At the time, he was our government-appointed driver. Said he was in jail for killing some people who 'deserved it'. He was very grateful to the senior local official who set him free and gave him employment. From then on, he said, he served—and went on committing more crimes—only at the behest of the island's head honcho.

When you're told such things, you do your best to keep your face emotionless. The storyteller was driving the car we were in and shared the information as if recounting a high school dance.

Then, there was the infamously bejewelled female official. Who was covered in baby powder and reeked of sticky perfume.

We bumped into her at some locale or other, and the moment we were introduced, she handed us CDs with music videos of her singing. Her assistant was carrying copies in a bag. I mean, it was *fascinating*—though, admittedly, some might call it insane.

And as careful as we were to not cause upset, a local contact raged against us because he felt mistreated. Apparently, we weren't grateful enough for his help. And he threatened me with bodily harm should I return to his island. It was not an un-terrifying experience.

But typically, there is no shortage of interesting people in such textured places. And all places are textured if you know how to look.

The Peace

Another time, we were in Sulu to speak with a newly appointed army general, who met us outside a mosque after Friday prayers. He was tasked by the national government to forge a peace with Muslim rebels. The same group of insurgents who had previously held him hostage.

Not that it's related, but it was after that experience that the general converted to Islam. An enlightened believer, he hoped his new faith would serve as a bridge.

It wasn't until years later that a peace deal was signed with so-called legitimate Muslim leaders. The Abu Sayyaf—extreme and ever opportunistic—was excluded from that agreement. And the group went on to pledge allegiance to the brutal Islamic State. Expecting that to bring in more money.

Despite the formal peace, the southern islands are still struggling to gain a foothold in the national narrative ... often still treated like outsiders in their own country.

Disinformation and mistrust persist, and the tapestry of the Philippines is a network of mangroves whose invisible roots remain tangled despite the outcrop.

And so, the islands' people keep hoping for a saviour to offer release from the stranglehold of poverty and desolation. Looking to autocratic rulers for redemption.

That optimistic military commander has retired, but private armed groups still run riot in their respective fiefdoms—which, frankly, is not just a problem for the southern islands. They're like viral infections on a long-infirm patient. Leaving putrid national flesh and rotting spirits.

The Forest for the Trees

This is the memory of that first trip to Sulu which still makes me shiver, and though forewarned of the risks, I was caught unprepared: we were in a troop transport truck—in the middle of the day—surrounded by heavy weapons and the governor's men. One of them looked at us and said: 'It's a good thing you are guests of the governor.' He spoke in the vernacular, so my British colleague was oblivious to what was said.

The armed man was smiling, and I thought it to be an opening for conversation. But before I could respond, he continued: 'Do you know how much each of you is worth?'

I immediately realized it was not a philosophical query. He wasn't referring to our value as human beings but as hostages whose ransom would change his life.

'Dollars'—he whispered with a glint in his eyes— 'we'd get dollars.'

It was terrifying and tragic. The commodification of humanity. An epidemic not limited to Sulu. After all this progress, what have we done to ourselves that everyone has a price, instead of seeing human life as priceless?

Where we were meant to be safe while in the thick of danger, the official shield was no guarantee of security. Just when we thought we recognized the good guys, the masks slipped off their faces. And conversely, even the feared had their fears.

I think of it as the teaching of the Palace of Flowers. That if you **dare to veer off the road,** you may **find the truth.**

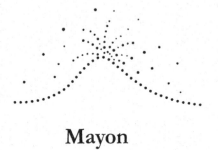

Mayon

IT'S STILL A CELEBRATION WITHOUT TINSEL.

Who would ever dream of spending Christmas at the foot of a volcano? To clarify: Christmas at the foot of not just any old volcano but the most active one in the Philippines—*while* lava is bubbling to the surface. Imagine an enormous overheating cauldron of deadly cheese fondue, as if it were the main offering at a Christmas banquet. Rivers of blood- red fire and treacly sunset hues.

In predominantly Christian Philippines, there is no more important religious festival than the birth of Jesus Christ. The place goes mad for it and boasts the longest Christmas season in the world. From the first of September, all the typical décor goes up—and then some. Trees draped in twinkling fairy lights. Capiz shell lanterns in every colour. Life-size figures of the full contingent making up the Biblical Nativity Scene: Baby Jesus, Joseph, Mary, the Three Kings, and the prerequisite bunch of sheep. Obviously, there are Santa Claus statues dressed in the standard red suit and sometimes in native garb. Huge shiny baubles, glitter, and tinsel. Plus, a flurry of fake snow. For three months leading up to December 25, people count down the days until they can open presents in the presence of their families and feast together on Christmas Eve with the largest meal of the year.

But in 2009, a province called Albay—which fronts the Pacific Ocean along the country's eastern coastline—was about to have a most unusual Christmas.

The Lady

Just as the Eiffel Tower defines the Paris skyline and the pyramids loom over Giza, Mayon Volcano lords over Albay's capital, Legazpi. At a height of nearly 2,500 metres, its near perfect cone can be seen from anywhere in the city.

From anywhere in seven other cities too actually. (There are eight that fan out from the base of the volcano.)

At the time, a quarter of a million people were living within ten kilometres of its crater.

Known for its conical symmetry, Mayon's name is derived from a local legend about a beautiful lady.

And Mayon truly is a thing of beauty. Its verdant, gentle slopes are often topped by a whisper of clouds. But this seemingly serene facade belies the raging fire that constantly churns within. In the last five hundred years, Mayon has erupted nearly fifty times, ranking it among the world's most explosive volcanos.

The Lady—as the locals call her—is also the centrepiece for a United Nations bio reserve, declared the country's first national park in 1936. A popular tourist destination.

And in December 2009, Mayon Volcano also made for a stunning Christmas tree—albeit crowned by a hazardous flame.

The Lot

Used to living in The Lady's volatile shadow, the agricultural community around the volcano wasn't easily frightened. They'd survived a major calamity three years earlier, when a super typhoon struck packing winds of up to 195 kilometres per hour. It caused floods, which brought boulders and all other built-up volcanic debris cascading down the slopes of Mayon. Burying villages, displacing tens of thousands, and killing more than one thousand people. The devastation was such that it prompted the national government to create a special agency dedicated to disaster preparedness and rapid response.

Al Jazeera had just launched, and this was the first major story we reported on out of the Philippines.

We drove overnight from Manila for more than twelve hours straight. Arriving in time to see the sun rise over Mayon. It was such a beautiful sight. Threads of gold, soft pinks, and salmon shadows, with just a wisp of steam rising from its crater. From that distance, you would never know the destruction that lay at its base.

This was just two years after I was in Iraq with CNN covering the war, but what we found in Albay was worse than I could have even imagined.

There was no power anywhere, and in many places, floodwaters were still high. Where they'd subsided, the acrid smell of volcanic sulphur mixed with the stench of death. I will never forget the pungency. It slid into your nostrils like acid, burning you raw from within. Each odour was fetid on its own. The combination was indescribably overwhelming.

People were buried in their homes or washed away by forceful waves of ash and mud. Local service workers—what remained of them—were bringing as many bodies as they could find to the morgues, but those soon overflowed. Corpses were laid out everywhere possible. Even on the grounds outside. Bloated, discoloured, and rigid. Frozen in the moment of death. It was heart-breaking to see survivors walk through the dead in search of their loved ones. I was so overcome that I had to step away and take a moment. My impulse was to call my parents. It's the only time I remember doing such a thing while working. My father answered the phone. He said he'd seen my report and asked how I was doing. I burst into tears. I don't think I said anything more. I just cried a most unfamiliar anguish. A minute later, I returned to work, to find our other colleague vomiting behind our vehicle. It was the first time any of us had seen so much death.

In Legazpi, Albay's provincial capital, hundreds of bodies were compiled in parks and at city hall, waiting for any claimants. Just metres from where we had to do our live reports. It was the only place that had a satellite signal.

So, three years later, in 2009, when Mayon's grumbling intensified again right before Christmas, the people of Legazpi were less anxious about it because there was no simultaneous storm. They were also more prepared.

Old hands by then at rapid emergency response, local officials evacuated tens of thousands of homes as soon as there were signs of an imminent eruption. There had been numerous earthquakes, lava flowing down the slopes like molasses, and jets of pyroclastic ash being spewed two kilometres into the air. Residents were already beginning to suffer skin irritation, vision problems, and having difficulty breathing.

In the run up to Christmas, people had to leave behind everything they owned, including their farms, their livestock, and any notion of celebrating the holidays traditionally. No Midnight Meal with the family, no singing carols, no presents. Seeking refuge when The Lady rumbled was not irregular, but they never had to do so at such a special time.

Again, our news team was in Legazpi. Hunkering down with our camera in the city's largest evacuation site: an old school, with a gym and an open-air basketball court. Prepared to bear witness to a very difficult Christmas for the hundreds of gathered residents.

But we couldn't have been more off base.

The Gift

As dusk descended, tiny lights began to flicker on the fruit trees and larger bulbs strobed in bold colours around the open-air basketball court. Ready for the dancing to start.

Yes, dancing.

'I'm so happy!' Ruth Espinas flashed me a bright, wide grin that rivalled the lights, repeating what turned out to be the night's chorus: 'We're happy, we're safe!' She laughed.

And the crowd around her laughed, too.

'We've had more food here than we could've hoped for had we stayed home'—they said—'and we didn't have to spend a cent.'

Small mercies considering the threat of an imminent volcanic eruption.

In one section of the schoolyard-turned-evacuation site, a clown entertained the children. In another, a massive white cloth was unfurled for a later film screening. And as night settled in, a DJ began to pump out his playlist. It thundered around us from huge black speakers. And I mean thundered. It's been more than a decade since and I can still feel the reverberations.

But as loud as it got, nothing could drown out the deafening sense of *joy*—which was not at all what one might expect of people again on the cusp of losing everything. For days—while waiting for the gurgling Lady to fully erupt—the people of Mayon lived with uncertainty, in the crowded discomfort of an evacuation centre.

Yet that Christmas Eve, instead of focusing on 'the bad', those gathered there found something for which to be thankful. As Ruth and her friends put it: they were forewarned and prepared, and they were with family. Safe, even if it was at an evacuation site. And—they added—the holiday fete was better than ever because the whole neighbourhood was there too, celebrating as one. With the bonus of the government picking up the tab.

'They sure know how to throw a party!' exclaimed another uncomplaining resident.

The Present

That Christmas Eve, those who lived around Mayon could celebrate because there were no casualties—and none were expected since they'd all sought refuge. Local officials were ready to keep evacuation centres running for as long as needed. And they threw the Christmas party to give people a breather from their woes.

'Life is kind,' another evacuee told me. 'God will take care of us.'

All the while, Mayon loomed evident in the black of night. Her viscous tendrils of fire crawling surely towards the town. Glowing like a treacherous sea of fairy lights funnelled through a network of streams.

'Have you ever seen anything like that?' I could hear the evacuees ask each other. 'What a beautiful sight!'

Never mind that the following morning could be catastrophic—they would deal with that then. What mattered was the present—and the present, as they saw it, wasn't too bad.

An Extraordinarily 'Typical' Christmas

This was the Christmas story of Mayon's residents that year. Unfettered joy and inextinguishable hope. A boundless celebration of the faith they had in God and in each other. Confident as they were of surviving whatever fate cast in their way. Even impending disaster.

As unusual as the situation was, it only heightened the spirit of the season—offering a light in the dark, with the expectation of a better year ahead.

The earth itself—they said—was providing them with 'natural' fireworks, as Mayon's lava continued to spill down its near perfect slopes.

'Look at that,' they called out to each other all night. 'What a beautiful sight!'

What a beautiful sight, indeed—when even the threat of calamity could not dampen a deep-seated trust in life's majesty.

I was away from my family that Christmas, but the people of Legazpi showed me that there's more to a burbling volcano than doom.

That Christmas Eve, I watched the residents of Mayon—who had already survived so much—raise their heads past molten rock and look to the stars, trusting in a greater Wisdom than their own. In the face of misfortune, they chose to hold on to a silver lining. No matter how faint it might have looked through all the ash.

Such sensibility isn't limited to the people of Albay. It was present across the Philippines' central islands after devastating floods turned millions of lives upside down. And in the country's south, despite freak typhoons leaving hundreds of people dead and thousands homeless.

It was evident too in Japan, after the horrendous earthquake and tsunami in 2011. Survivors of natural calamities understood there was much to do for recovery, but they looked gratefully towards an inevitable spring and the hope it brought for renewal.

Witnessing the strength of all these people helped me through my most difficult Christmas several years later—when I lost my mother in the middle of such a joyous season. As Manila prepared to celebrate, she slipped away from illness. To the very end, cared for by family. I knew how fortunate that made us. That we who survived her could be there for her and had each other to lean on. Which was more than could be said for so many others who experienced such epic catastrophes.

It might sound simplistic, but what else can you do when confronted with tragedy? **Find strength in something you can be grateful for**.

What survivors have shown me is that, ultimately, they get through because they trust the rhythm of life, and always—always—**there are the stars**.

THE WESTERN PACIFIC

Micronesia

SOMETIMES, PARADISE ISN'T.

There were so many things I did not know about the Micronesian islands. One: exactly where they were. Two: how many of them there might have been. They're barely visible on any world map. Especially in those scaled to size. You could even think them just specks of dust on a vast blue sea. Blink, and you might miss them.

So, when my long-time colleague was about to relocate from the Philippines in 2013, it was perfect that our final assignment together took us to the one place in the Asia Pacific region that neither of us had been: Micronesia.

It was rarely in the news, but that didn't mean there wasn't anything newsworthy about it—its meagre size belies its geopolitical importance. Which would also explain why despite its fine beaches and crystalline waters, you don't see it among the usual list of beach paradise hot spots.

Strewn in a vital Pacific corridor between Asia and America, the islands have seen more military hardware than sunscreen, swimsuits, and straw hats.

Small But ...

In preparing for the trip, I learnt that Micronesia—Greek for 'small isles'—is made up of some 2,000 islands and atolls, grouped into four main archipelagos. Divided further into five different countries (Palau, Nauru, Marshall Islands, FSM or Federated States of Micronesia, and Kiribati) and three US territories (Guam, the Northern Marianas, and Wake Island). All of them shimmer shyly in the tropical sun like gems scattered from a broken bracelet.

Super small and surrounded by water, they're not easy to get to. Any trip over is neither straightforward nor cheap.

From Manila, we had to fly to Guam—the US territory that is also the largest of the islands. At about 541 square kilometres, it's three-fourths the size of Singapore. From there, we hopscotched to the destinations of our choice. Making sure we arrived on the right day for a connecting flight. There's normally only one a week. Otherwise, you have to wait. Which we learnt is a favourite pastime on the islands.

Island Time

Time, in Micronesia, has its own rhythm. The islands stand apart from manic twenty-first-century reality, and don't seem in any hurry to catch up with the rest of the world.

Days are languid and warm. With mornings as crisp as the waters from young coconuts and afternoons sweet as mango.

As beautiful as you might imagine.

Each Micronesian entity boasts a particular closeness to the US and are under various degrees of its protection.

Why? Because the islands are in a stretch of ocean that is passed through by majority of global trade. Trillions of dollars' worth between East and West. And it's been said that whoever holds sway over Micronesia controls the mighty Pacific.

Closer to China than the US, both those superpowers have been jockeying for influence over the area for years. The US has been ahead on that front since World War II, with significant military bases in Guam, but with China's growing might and undeniable economic power, things could change … in a blink.

See-En-Em-Eye

That's how the locals refer to the Commonwealth of the Northern Mariana Islands, the northernmost of the archipelagos. As if the abbreviation were a single word. C-N-M-I. A group of fourteen small islands in the north-western Pacific Ocean that is an 'unincorporated territory and commonwealth' of the US. Self-administered like one of its fifty states, but not part of the federal union. Same as the better-known Puerto Rico.

Regardless of the official term, CNMI is technically— ironically—the last colony of the world's self-styled guardian of democracy.

Again, closer to China than mainland US, the currency is the greenback dollar, food portions in its restaurants are as large as they are on 'the mainland', and the license plates on its cars loudly declare: 'CNMI–USA'.

The residents (population barely 50,000) are also US citizens— but with limited rights. They can serve in the US military, for example, but not vote for president.

And most people living on CNMI are migrants, with barely any rights at all. But we'll get to that shortly.

The Locals

Chamorros and Carolinians are the indigenous groups. They take pride in being seen as peaceful, unassertive, and easy-going. Both were colonized by Europeans for centuries, which led to the diminishment of their populations. Though now intermingled, each has a unique culture and heritage. The Chamorros are thought to have come from Indonesia and the Philippines in Southeast Asia, while the Carolinians—who call themselves the 'People of the Deep Sea'— are believed to have travelled from Oceania.

Only the indigenous can own land in CNMI. Anyone else can just get a lease unless they claim descent.

The CNMI locals speak in a slow cadence with undeniable North American accents. And though they also fall under the category of 'Austronesians' like the Samoans further east, they are not the same.

Why am I going on about them? I just want to give them their due, since many who have never been to the islands are barely aware that such distinct ethnicities exist among Pacific Islanders.

As unhurried as life was when we got to CNMI, it nearly wasn't so.

Land of Missed Opportunities

In the 1980s, the territory opened to skilled migrant workers. Investments poured in from China and Japan, and the economy boomed. Manufacturers and garment factories were everywhere, and the service industry was preparing for it to be the next Hawaii. Large resorts sprouted up spruced in pastel like sets for *Miami Vice*.

Workers came in droves from nearby Philippines.

'I even brought a jacket,' recalled Philippine-born Rudy Francisco, confessing his naïve atmospheric expectations of 'being in the US'.

It was supposed to be the land of promise and dreams-come-true, he shared, bitter-sweet.

He was wrong.

'It's amazing what few friends you have when you lose everything.'

When we met him in 2013, Rudy had been living in Saipan, the largest of the Northern Mariana Islands, for over twenty years. Like many other migrant workers, he lost his job in the early 2000s. Factories closed and moved to cheaper pastures

in Southeast Asia. He couldn't find new employment, and
worse, he was still waiting to be paid for his last job. He had
no savings and was owed over US$60,000 in back wages. On
top of all this, he no longer had documents to stay in CNMI.
A place he'd lived in longer than the land of his birth.

It's a story shared by many migrants. Most of whom toiled
with barely any pay under conditions akin to slavery. They'd hoped
that the US connection to CNMI would improve their lot, but the
nuts and bolts of migrant labour laws were left at the discretion
of the island government. And the island government didn't want
'guests'—which is what the foreign workers were called regardless
of how long they'd lived in CNMI—benefitting from their US
social services.

Since then, several local officials have been accused of
corruption and suspected of having ties with unscrupulous
Chinese businesses. One of them was convicted—but plagued by
health woes, his sentence was commuted, and he disappeared to the
Philippines where he had access to private care in a luxury hospital.

Meanwhile, Rudy was stuck in limbo on CNMI. Living in
a grass shack, hidden from view behind forest overgrowth. A
phantom whose paradise dream had turned into a nightmare.

'It's embarrassing how easily I trusted things would go right,'
he admitted.

The lasting image I have of Rudy is him sitting alone on a
bench on a deserted stretch of beach, staring out at the ocean.
Along with his ill-fitting, unwashed clothes, he wore the haunted
gaze of a trauma survivor. And frozen on his face—the turmoil
of the tears he refused to shed.

Hop, Chew, and a Yap

Another thing I learnt: paperwork means little in paradise. There
are other means of binding agreements. Let me expound.

From CNMI, we headed on to Yap, an even smaller island
where we were greeted at the airport by women wearing only

grass skirts. They smiled warmly and put a garland of flowers around our necks.

Yap—all forty-six square miles of it—is of volcanic origin, consisting of four small main islands separated by narrow waterways. The grouping is surrounded by outlying atolls, one of four states that comprise the Federated States of Micronesia (FSM). An independent country, and different to CNMI.

Yap has no industry to speak of bar traditional wood carving and marine tourism. There were only a handful of visitors when we were there, and other than subsistence farming and fishing, locals relied on aid from the US to survive.

CNMI's capital Saipan was slow, but it was Manhattan compared to Yap's Colonia.

Even the people moved in slow motion. If you placed a call, it *might* get answered on the tenth try. For no other reason than the person on the receiving end (a government agency) was listening to the radio.

There was no public transport system on Yap, and if you needed a ride, you had to make sure there wasn't a football match on, or no one would come get you. No one. Not even if you promised to pay them a day's wage.

In that sense, it seemed money meant little to the Yapese. True wealth on the island was measured by the size of the stone coins you owned. Yes, stone 'coins'. Giant ones. Known as Rai, some of the coins were four metres in diameter and weighed more than a car. They were displayed in front of homes or alongside roads. But this didn't necessarily mean that the Rai belonged to the owners of the land they were on.

The coins had a hole in the centre from when the stones were originally brought over as far back as the twelfth century from Palau, where they were quarried. That's a distance of some 240 nautical miles.

Carved out of limestone, their value came from the community's shared belief in it.

Yes, *belief* made it so.

Once in place, the weighty Rai was difficult to move, so when ownership was exchanged, an oral ledger was used to keep track. Everyone knew when transactions were made. It's a system of valuation and ownership that economists have studied for years, and it even serves as the basic principle for cryptocurrency. I kid you not. Trust. And community agreement.

Speaking of trust, while on Yap, we had to *trust* that we would be fed. Despite a printed menu, meals at the hotel were dependent on what fishermen caught that day, and if they didn't go out to sea, then we had vegetables. If no vegetables had been harvested, there were always canned goods. (Thank goodness for SPAM!)

Other than vegetables for their own consumption, many Yapese grew betel nut for sale. It seemed everyone on the island was chewing it. Even the children. We saw some as young as five years old roll their own betel quids to chew on, as fast as they might play with marbles.

We were there at a time when the island was anxious about losing its access to US aid. Ripe for those offering them a new source of income.

And who came knocking? A neighbour who'd become one of the world's largest economies.

Doing Business in Yap

Aside from our news team and a development worker from an international bank, there was just one other guest at what was technically the only resort in town. A Chinese businessman. Every day, we saw him come and go with a briefcase. Not in shorts or flip-flops, and no sunglasses. He was clearly not on holiday. Every afternoon, he returned looking worse for wear. We were told he'd been in and out of Yap going on two years.

Two years trying to get any of the locals to lease him their land. Most of the property on Yap is privately owned—and by law, the Yapese are not allowed to sell to outsiders.

The Chinese businessman worked for a company that was planning to build a ten-thousand room golf resort. On tiny little Yap. With its rugged terrain, fringing reefs, and rising sea levels. Not to mention its coastline of mangrove forests.

No one believed the Chinese businessman. In the time we were there, the planned ten-thousand-room resort was redesigned to only host five thousand rooms. This was further altered and downsized to a thousand five hundred. Many of the locals were convinced that the Chinese were actually mapping a military installation. A counterbalance to the US armed presence on nearby Guam. And the Yapese didn't want to get caught in the crossfire of a geopolitical struggle between superpowers.

At the time, only one family was considering leasing their land to the Chinese company. But it was such a small plot that the company's rep said it was virtually useless to him. He wouldn't speak to us on camera, but his exasperation was discernible. He was ready to throw in the towel—but his company didn't want to have to send a new rep out to start from scratch to try and win over the locals.

It's been 10 years since … and still no 'golf resort'. As I understand it, the Chinese are still in Yap trying to get it done. Perhaps their patience will pay off—it was foretold that whoever put in the most money would eventually win out.

Yes, *foretold*. We met a soothsayer on Yap, the 'magic man', he was called. He was the only one giving import to any *papers*—the tarot cards he used to read the future.

And despite the predicted windfall, he didn't necessarily have any visions of paradise.

And Then, There's the Haunted Paradise

A short prop-plane-ride away lay another surprise, Tinian. With land area equivalent to Paris or twice the size of Manhattan, the undeveloped Tinian is part of the CNMI chain. Another beautiful

Micronesian island whose growth has been caught between its strategic location and its history.

In World War II, it was from Tinian that US planes took off to drop atomic bombs on Japan. Marking the end of the conflict. For decades after, most of the island's visitors were war vets. And there was little else on Tinian by way of livelihood.

Less than three-thousand people call the island home—and they'd only been allowed to return to it after the war. The US military had leased two-thirds of the land for ninety-nine years, and they used it mostly for war games. They were meant to build a military base—which the islanders welcomed as a source of income.

But said base was never installed, and what should have become a bustling town remained nothing more than an empty field. In the only paved section, there was a signpost: Broadway corner Wall Street. Not too far from it, a marker with a map that mirrored Manhattan. A blueprint for the Tinian city that never got built. Patterned after the dynamic cosmopolitan island in New York.

There was one main road on Tinian, with a general store that was the spot for 'people watching'. If you were lucky, you might catch 'rush hour'—the only time of day that a car drove past. I waited. But wouldn't you know it—I blinked at just the wrong moment and missed it!

Investors were being courted to the island with US residence permits. If they put down a certain amount, they were offered a much-coveted green card. Tinian, of course, being part of CNMI. Unincorporated US territory and all that. The only development we spotted were resorts being built by Chinese companies.

'I'll take their investment over ammunition,' one resident told us.

When we were there, the US was planning to conduct live fire drills in some of the island's most abundant areas. Much to the locals' dismay. They were already fenced out of fishing grounds.

'Is that what we're good for? Target practice?'

A group of concerned residents was suing the US military, but the case seemed headed nowhere. Such is the plight of small island territories. They're shunted about with little import given to their sovereignty or their well-being. Larger, wealthier countries can—and have—literally removed people from where they live. If not for military reasons, then through the damages wrought by climate change, which has been exacerbated by the big, industrialized nations. Increasingly strong storms and rising sea levels means island states have to battle not just flooding but tidal surges that eat away at their coastline. Then, there's the destruction of their marine biosystems.

Those who live on these Pacific islands have no choice but to consider options for when their home disappears. And on CNMI, many wondered how things ended up as they are when they're meant to be under the protection of the United States. The global guardian of human rights.

The islanders said they felt like second-class US citizens—and the migrants were treated like second-class islanders.

Someone's big fish is always someone else's little fish.

Palau and the Push-and-Pull

Another independent country among the Micronesians, Palau is an archipelago of some 300 coral and volcanic islands, half enclosed by a large barrier reef that stretches for almost 115 kilometres. Its terrain was like nothing I'd ever seen. There were hundreds of raised coral 'rock islands' that looked like verdant mushrooms rising out of the turquoise sea. And to the north, the most inhabited islands were linked by a steel bridge and a causeway. It only took minutes to cross the combined eighteen-square-kilometre area.

But again, its beauty was deceptive. The Palauans we met were already struggling with soil erosion and the rising salination of what little arable land there was. That's why we were there. Their government was looking to sue industrial nations for climate change damages—but like Tinian, their case seemed to be headed nowhere.

At the time, barely 8,000 people lived in Palau. Among its colourful residents were persons under witness protection from other countries and those running from international criminal syndicates. It seemed easy to disappear in a place like that—where no one asks for your full name or needs to know why you're really there.

Like the rest of Micronesia, Palau was—is—stunning. A veritable paradise. But as remote and idyllic as it seems, its very existence is at the mercy of larger—wealthier—more powerful entities. Just as it is for every small nation on the planet.

Like Rudy and all other 'undocumented' migrants, caught in impossible, political tugs-of-war. Subject to the whims of unsympathetic giants.

But what I learnt in Micronesia is one survives by standing their ground, and **holding on to what matters** despite the waves. Like **trust**, and **faith**, and **community**. Then, even if paradise proves to be challenging, you can persist.

THE MIDDLE EAST

Baghdad

SOME PEOPLE NEVER AGE.

There are moments in life that change us forever. That become markers on our journey to the end. I spent about a year going in and out of Iraq on long assignments for CNN, just after the US invasion in 2003 that toppled its leader, Saddam Hussein. Occupied by Western forces and without a head of state, the country descended into chaos. It was a 'story' that news careers are built on. An extraordinary time that shaped not just the journalist I became, but the person I am.

When I recall Baghdad now, it is always in tones of russet and bronze. The colour of sepia and dusk, through a veil of timeless shamal sandstorms.

The hue of the copious cups of native cardamom chai we drank in the bureau.

A Dream Come True

Before Iraq, I had never been in an active warzone. It's not usually a scenario that's up there when pondering the future.

But looking back, had I the chance then to actually consider it, I would have been glad to go with those I was with. There was no better group—nor news team more lauded—to be with in Baghdad than CNN. The network made its reputation in the early '90s on its coverage of the first Gulf War. And I got my start in news watching the channel and re-cutting their stories for viewers in the Philippines. To get to work, twelve years later, with those same people I'd admired—well, it was astounding. There was no greater goal then for a young journalist like me than to be a part of CNN.

High Spirits and a Drag Show

As news assignments go, I was in Iraq on a fluke. I happened to be standing by the newsdesk in London when the call came in that 'another body' was needed on the ground. The reporter in Baghdad at the time knew me—so thanks to her vouching for my work, two hours later, I had rushed home, packed a bag, and was in a company cab to Heathrow airport to catch the first flight to Jordan.

I landed in the capital, Amman, at 1 a.m. to a message that I was to be on a network convoy leaving the city at 4 a.m. sharp. Everything was carefully timed as we needed to meet an outgoing convoy from Baghdad at the Iraqi–Jordanian border. Passengers would be exchanged, then we would be driven across the country to get to the Iraqi capital before nightfall and curfew.

Well, it was a weekend, and wouldn't you know it, there was a workers' strike at Heathrow. My suitcase—along with half the plane's cargo—was left in the terminal. None of us passengers waiting in Amman were informed until what few bags did arrive were gone from the conveyor belt. We stood there just waiting for about an hour. Thank goodness they eventually found the bag that contained my flak jacket and helmet. But my clothing was still sitting in London. The airline assured me that my suitcase would get in that Monday, which would be grand except there was no way for it to then be transported to Iraq. It would have to wait in Amman until the next security convoy was scheduled. Which was not for at least another week.

By the time I left the airport, it was almost 3 a.m., and I had forty-five minutes to 'freshen up' at the hotel before needing to leave on this convoy.

It was an eleven-hour drive through the desert, and I wore my flak jacket and helmet from the moment we crossed the border into Iraq. We passed towns that were hubs of insurgency against US forces. And the closer we got to Baghdad, the more signs there were of the war and the occupation. Thick concrete blast walls, barbed wire fences, heavily guarded checkpoints. Streets and structures pockmarked by ammunition. Military vehicles, bombed-out buildings, and mountains of rubble.

Once past the final checkpoint and blast barriers, I walked into the Baghdad bureau just as dusk descended, wearing all I had: the clothes on my back, a flak jacket, and a helmet. The reporter—the only other female in the office then—offered to lend me some clothing, which was lovely but frankly she was half my size! So instead, she loaned me some money and asked one of the locals to take me shopping for clothes.

Bless the poor man who drove me. We went everywhere, but all the women's shops were closed that late in the day. The only place we could find open was a men's sporting store. Where I proceeded to get a week's worth of shirts and shorts. The only things there that fit me.

Fortunately, on the way back to where we were staying, we chanced upon this itty-bitty hole in the wall that sold women's undergarments. Since I don't speak Arabic, the driver had to come into the store with me. I had known the man for all of five minutes—and there he was having to help me buy some bras and knickers! Just imagine our discussion on sizing. Yes, it was as uncomfortable (and hilarious) as you might imagine. The poor guy couldn't look me in the eye for weeks.

After this hullabaloo, I returned to our battle-scarred hotel to find I'd been put up in a massive suite with a lounge/kitchen area and two huge bedrooms. The space was understandably rundown but seemed functional. It was previously occupied by the chap I was replacing.

As soon as I dropped off my shopping, I re-joined my colleagues in the makeshift bureau behind the hotel.

I didn't finish work until past two that morning, and I returned to my prized lodging to discover that it had absolutely no toilets. I mean, nothing. Where the two—yes, two!—separate water closets were, there was only a hole in the floor and pipes sticking out of the wall.

So, I trekked back down to reception hoping for a room change.

The overnight manager insisted I was mistaken.

'So many doors in your suite,' he reiterated. 'You must look.'

I smiled, and he sent me back up with a huge security guard who was meant to prove him right. A few minutes later, we were back at reception. The security guard was flushed (pardon the pun), apologising profusely, and telling the manager the suite was indeed *sans* toilet.

Unsure of what to expect in a warzone, I was just glad to get a bed to sleep in—but with everyone else having a loo in their rooms, surely, I could ask for one too, no?

They gave me another room. And I finally got to use a toilet before the sunrise.

That was my first day in Iraq.

For the next two weeks—because it took longer than expected for the airline to get me my suitcase—I looked like a displaced Aussie surfer in my new line of oversized sporty men's wear. The bureau manager kept me on desk duty so I wouldn't have to be seen in public. But every time I walked through the lobby and the hotel grounds to the bureau, I inevitably encountered at least one Iraqi man wearing the same shirt as I had on.

And one of those men became a dear, dear friend.

Behind the Headlines

His name was Duraid. A twenty-seven-year-old father of two. One of the best producers CNN had in Baghdad. Along with another young colleague called Odai, we became a little trio. And it was working with them that drove home the point that news reporting is heavily reliant on local producers and teamwork. It wasn't just the coverage but our lives that depended on that.

Whip smart, charming, and intuitive, Duraid taught me how to read between the lines on assignment. A necessary skill especially in a setting where fiction was often passed off as fact. From him, I learnt not to take everything I read or heard as truth.

If Duraid said something was so, he was usually right. So, more than anything, I learnt to trust his instincts.

That year, after insurgents fired rockets at our hotel, I got time off over Christmas and flew to see family in Manila. I wasn't scheduled to be back in Baghdad until the end of January.

Enterprising as they were, Duraid and Odai got hold of a landline number to reach me in the Philippines. They called to send holiday wishes and ask if I might consider returning to Iraq earlier than planned. Duraid was being assigned to a military embed when I was scheduled to arrive, and they had hoped to catch up in person before then.

There is something about such intense assignments that gets under your skin. Maybe it's the ephemerality of life, the immediacy of mortality. Everything is heightened so even the ties you forge are stronger. I didn't need to think twice about cutting my holiday short and returning to work. At that point, I felt like half a person away from it. It gave me a sense of purpose. I was feeling more comfortable—and useful—in Baghdad than I did elsewhere. And yes, I have heard it likened to a sort of Stockholm Syndrome.

I will forever be grateful that the guys called that day and I returned to work early. Duraid was killed in an ambush before the end of the month. Just seven days after I got back to Baghdad.

I had never lost a friend before. Especially to such violence.

I remember every second of that day. And if I shut my eyes, I can replay it all in slow motion. I remember how my heart stopped when we got the call that a CNN convoy had been ambushed. The car that Duraid and Yasser—who was driving— were in had been separated from the group.

I remember the succeeding hours when I was certain they survived the chase and were just hiding somewhere waiting out the attackers.

I remember when the call eventually came in that a vehicle was found run off the road … there were two young men in it that had not survived a hail of bullets.

I remember Odai's voice hours later, when after going to check, he confirmed that those found dead in the car were indeed Duraid and Yasser.

I remember the shock and the chaos that descended upon us in the bureau. It was like being in suspended animation. I went numb. I was present—but not. I knew what was happening—but I was in stasis. The pain was so great I couldn't feel it. You know when something is so hot that it feels cold, and vice versa? It was like that.

But there was news to be broadcast and stories to be written. And our headquarters in the States needed to be told about the deadly ambush. Instinctively, I felt I had no alternative but to focus on work. I *had* to be useful. At that point, it felt like there was no space for feelings. I learnt that such a response seems par for the course for many people when in similar positions.

It was the first time that CNN had suffered such a loss. And I will never forget how awful it was to speak to bereaved families.

I don't think I can write it all down for you, though. The jumble that was that day. Suffice it to say that despite the grief and the horror, we had to keep going. And maybe it was the need to carry on that kept us from falling apart.

We were all offered counselling and an early end to our tours of duty, but every one of us from the international team chose to stay in Baghdad. It made more sense to be able to grieve with people who understood. We would've just felt cut off and isolated had we left.

So, I stayed for two more months. Until the news manager convinced me I needed to take a break.

In those months—full of breaking news and the constant need to broadcast—we all had to find pockets of time to deal with our emotions.

I used to lock myself in my room, draw the curtains shut, and listen to an instrumental CD my mother had given me. It was called *Silence*. A collection of soulful, instrumental music. I found it soothing to not have to deal with words.

In those few, brief moments, I sat in the dark alone and wept. Allowing myself to feel everything that I held back in the harsh light of the desert day.

And then, I pulled myself together to return to the world outside.

Years later, one of the other producers who was there with us thanked me. I thought it was an odd thing to say, which I expressed to him. He then recounted to me that on the day of the ambush—as he remembered it—I 'held it together'. He said he saw me work the newsdesk, field calls, and deal with colleagues' anxious relatives, despite what he described as my palpable grief. At one point, he said, I put the phone down and cried, thinking that no one could see me. But it was seeing me—he recounted—that let him feel it was ok to mourn. To let sorrow in and be vulnerable.

According to him, after that moment, I sat back up, wiped my eyes, and returned to work. It was January 2004. The news didn't stop out of Iraq, and we had to get on with it.

Flashback

This brings back the memory of a separate incident involving one of our news managers. A little boy battling leukaemia was brought to the bureau by his father. The father was clearly heartbroken. They needed to get the boy out of Iraq for medical treatment, but no one was giving them the necessary exit papers.

It was not a news story, and we were not an NGO, but as human beings, how could you not help an ailing child?

So, we did what we could behind the scenes, connecting the family with the right agencies to get the boy the help he needed.

For several days, father and son sat with us in the bureau, just waiting for their hope to bear fruit. We gave them endless cups of tea, fed them what there was, and took turns keeping them company.

One day, a call came in for the bureau manager and I couldn't find her. She had the desk across from me and never left her seat, but this time, she wasn't there. After searching everywhere, I came upon her in a quiet corner of the locker room-turned-makeshift tape library. (These were the days when we still used videotapes, and the 'office' was actually an emptied hotel pool house protected by a sandbag barrier.)

So, there in that poorly lit space was the news manager, hunched over towards the wall, hiding her face. This seasoned journalist, famously made of steel, was in tears. She was not happy to see me.

'Are you ok?' I asked, timidly.

'This place will break your heart,' she said, softly. 'Over and over again. It will break your heart.'

I had never seen her like that.

'Sometimes, you have to let yourself feel it,' she said as she wiped away her tears.

It's not what I expected. I thought she would tell me that as journalists we had to harden ourselves and not get involved. But I was wrong.

This incredibly strong woman and kick-ass news manager then straightened her shoulders and put her emotions back in check.

'You never saw this,' she said. And returned to the workspace.

Why am I recounting this? She will not be pleased, but I wanted to say that I respected her even more after that. Though I was supposed to pretend it never happened, seeing her like that was such a powerful reminder that as journalists, we should never forget our humanity.

But we also mustn't let it interfere with the job at hand.

As witnesses to other people's reality—we should never take the focus for ourselves.

Wailing Winds

It was in Iraq that I first heard the gut-wrenching wailing of people in the throes of pain. Literally. Every time they received news of someone being killed, they beat on their chests, crying out and screaming wherever they were. Like feral creatures fighting for survival. Such ululation rips through your skin and seeps into your bones, crushing the arid wind out of your chest.

And it was not the last place that I was overwhelmed by the sound of heartbreak. It is universal. You do not need to understand the language of the words when the shriek the yell the tone the texture of the anguish is the same. Deafening in its torment. So raw in its nakedness that you want to turn away so as not to see it—but you can't. It is inescapable. You cannot shut your eyes to existential howling.

There is no running away from pain when it surrounds you. Like a welcoming embrace, it grips you to its bosom and suffocates.

On the Page

Being in Iraq was not easy, but it was also a most enriching period. And one of the clearest memories I have. Down to how my skin felt and how things smelled.

I will never forget Duraid and Yasser. Or Charles and Marla. Two others killed in Iraq who we knew quite well in the bureau. One was a civilian working in communications for coalition forces, and the other was a human rights activist turned aid worker.

There are thousands of others more who died in a senseless war. And the futility of armed conflict, I carry with me always.

When I recall Iraq, even the good days are tinged with profound sadness—a constant reminder that many people don't get to age past their youth.

Duraid was twenty-seven when he was taken, full of dreams for his two young sons and his broken nation. It was the reason he worked with CNN at the risk of being called a traitor by his people. Like many others who worked with international agencies, Duraid was fighting for their voices to be heard when the story of their nation was told.

What follows is something I wrote in the silence of my Baghdad room a few days after he was killed. Do allow me to share it with you.

1 February 2004
Sunday, 2038, Baghdad

> The radio continues to crackle in the background.
>
> 'Ahmed, Ahmed where are you? Live shot in five minutes. N—, N—, are you in your room—over. *Isti'ilamat—isti'ilamat...*'

I hear my watch ticking incessantly on the nightstand and I have put on a CD—ironically called *Silence*—to try to drown out this place.

This place …

The Bradleys haven't started rolling outside my window yet. The overnight shift at the checkpoint hasn't arrived to replace the dayside contingent.

The mortars haven't been launched—and the IEDs are still silent.

It is early. The explosions will start soon enough. The rumbling that shakes the very core of you—from inside out almost. The tracer fire … the wailing sirens … it is nearly nine o'clock. Attack time. Another night in Baghdad.

I am sitting in a time bomb. This place is a time bomb. What hope I had that all would only get better has dissipated. They killed Duraid—and suddenly Baghdad is no longer welcoming. It's gone insane. It is an angry, volatile place—and without Saddam and with Bush far away, people no longer know who the enemy is. They don't have a target for their hatred and their frustration and their grief—so they're killing anyone they can.

It is a family dispute gone haywire—and I am just a stranger looking in. How dare I? How dare I be here to witness their pain? I feel like an intruder in an otherwise honourable home—I shouldn't be here to see their shame.

It is a country ready to implode—and I shouldn't be here like a parasite taking advantage of their tragedy because it will make the nightly news.

BOOM!

One.

And it isn't even nine-o-clock yet. They started early tonight. Ten minutes early.

I no longer even run to see what it is. I no longer care.

I no longer care if we get it on the air first.

I no longer care that we get the pictures or the story—let these people get on with their lives.

How dare we journalists watch their misery just to slap a few shots together to make a good package and then call it a day?

Because that is what we end up doing: we go from story to story, and then we call it a day. Maybe, just maybe, some of us go on to write that bestselling book about our voyeuristic experiences and take down tyrannical governments with exposes. Is that the happily ever after?

Can I live like that?

It was different for Duraid. In many ways, he _was_ the story. He was Iraq. Its future. Its hope. Its heartbeat. Angry enough to take risks. Smart enough to still be cautious. Jaded enough to not be foolish—but with enough pride and hope to <u>believe</u> that things would get better if he only took that one more step forward.

One more step. One foot in front of the other—and he would get <u>there</u>. Wherever THERE may be.

Duraid believed in his country more than anyone I've ever met. He believed he deserved better—that his family deserved better—so he always gave 101%, expecting that somewhere out there, it would be given back to him.

But his own people put a bullet through his head.

I can't even bear to think about it. I don't want to think about it—but part of me believes I should. I should piece it all together in my head like a newsreel, so it'll become 'real'. Oh, the irony in that! Can I only see things as real now if they are captured on tape?

But I must make this real. Because if not, I sit here at times complacently, expecting him to walk through the door with that confident jaunt—a pack of red 'Marlies' stuffed into his back pocket ... his glasses sliding down his nose ... beads of sweat dripping down his forehead (even in the winter) ... a cigarette hanging loosely from his lips ... and a sly, cheeky smile spread securely on his bright, bright face ... his laptop held tightly under one arm ... and a surprise package of Oreos for 'Gamra'—which is what they call me—hidden under the other.

Sometimes, it would be a secret stash of M&Ms.

He teased me about my perpetual failed diet—but then, he played a large part in its failure.

Duraid, always rushing into the office with something for someone.

But often, it was black market goodies for me.

Through the quotidian horrors of war, people here keep smiling. The irony. In a place that has to confront tragedy daily, there is still such faith that life can only get better.

It has to get better. People here are exhausted—it is tangible. But they move forward, one foot in front of the other, with dignity and grace. Shattered spirits holding themselves together with honour.

How do I explain my ties to Baghdad? I can't. Many people don't get it. How could you put yourself in danger, they first wondered. But I never saw it like that.

It's funny—these out-of-town assignments. They create a different kind of bond between colleagues—an intense energy that links you, one with the other, and fast forms a surrogate family. You put your lives in each other's hands ... and you have to build instant trust. It is almost instinct.

My God, what are we doing?

BOOM. BOOM. BOOM.

Not as loud as the first one. Twenty-two minutes past nine. Sounds like mortar fire. I think. I am learning to tell the difference now. No sirens in the background. So, they can't have landed in the Green Zone.

Just a few days ago, I was playing backgammon with Duraid in the new rest area. He was clearly an old hand, a master at this game. But I beat him. I beat him fair and square.

Or he let me win.

Then again, it's all in the roll of the die, isn't it? If you get the snake-eyes, there's not much you can do about it.

More banging. I don't think this is artillery fire. Sounds like hammering at a construction site. Another regular sound in this town. They are—after all—trying to rebuild.

There are just too many sounds here at night. Not crickets or owls or even buzzing insects. Not any of the gentle tones romantics associate with evenfall.

In Baghdad, the night resonates with noises human beings really shouldn't have to deal with on a regular basis. Man-made excursions on the road to self-destruction.

Darkness was always a tender friend—but I don't trust it anymore. You never know what ugliness will face you in the morning after nightfall in Baghdad.

This was supposed to be about Duraid. Forgive me—my self-indulgent rant has once again turned back in on its

narrator. How has this come to be about my no longer
feeling like I can do the 'news'? How I no longer know
how to remain 'detached' from the 'reality' I am supposed
to be 'covering'?

'Covering'. There. That word alone sums up the entire
profession. We like to think we are separate, or at least one-
removed, from a 'story'—observing and putting together
beginning, middle, and end. Structure. Denouement. We hide
behind our cameras and our microphones. Like swords and
shields. We are but <u>witnessing</u> what happens to other people.
How have I forgotten that? I feel like I was in a cocoon. A
safe bubble from which I could watch the world go by and
never have it touch me.

But someone's put a bullet through my windowpane—and
now, there is no escaping the hurricane outside.

The wind is literally howling. Truly, it is. Rather fitting that
on the day we visit Yasser's family to offer our condolences,
a freak thunderstorm rolls across Baghdad. I've never heard
thunder like that—and I grew up in the tropics.

And then there's the rain.

I never realized how it could rain in the desert.

I know Duraid, I know. I am an ignorant fool. There was
so much I was looking forward to learning from you. You
understood this place like no one does. Like an insider
looking out to look in again. You could speak our language to
help us understand, and your heart was rooted firmly on the
Tigris riverbed.

My radio crackles to life beside me.

'Gamra ... Gamra ... where are you?'

On any other night, it would have been Duraid calling.

'Gamra … Gamra … *wenek?*' Our little group's code for 'time-to-get-out-of-the-office-and-chill-in-the-DVD-room'.

But this time it is Odai on the radio. Dear, dear Odai.

We are all in mourning—he more than me, I'm sure.

It gives me comfort to think he might need me around. I don't think he knows being around him helps me, too.

'Gamra—Gamra—please come see me,' he calls, again.

Above, the Black Hawks begin to circle the night sky. I can hear them. For the first time, I am sitting here with my back to the window—like I can no longer bear to look outside.

Silence ends. I must go see Odai.

Evening in Baghdad.

My radio continues to crackle.

'Isti'ilamat … Isti'ilamat …'

BOOM.

* * *

For years after that, those of us who were there would ring each other up across the globe on the anniversary of the ambush. To check in, to remember, to grieve.

For years.

And what did it teach me? In Iraq, I learnt that the only way to get past something is to go through it. That you must trust yourself and let yourself feel whatever it is you feel. Emotions are like fireflies—they shine a light and shouldn't be bottled up.

Or ignored in hopes they disappear.

The best way forward is to gently take a step into your jungle, and face down whatever gnarly darkness is before you. Even without a torch or a map, just keep going until a path reveals itself.

Or pause and wait until the sun comes out. Either way, there is no pretending that what is painful is not happening. You can try to bury it deep until scabs grow over the wound—but if it doesn't heal, the smallest of pricks can make it bleed again. And the pain ... the pain will be even greater than you imagined.

So, there's no need to expel energy trying to find ways around, above, or underneath it—just go through the thicket and you will see yourself in a whole new light on the other side.

Final Note

Some people don't get to live past twenty-seven, so you have a duty to yourself to **give it all you've got.**

You are here—and you are alive.

Grief and pain may be indefatigable lurkers, but they won't be as startling if you leave the light on and let them in for tea.

Suleimaniyah

You may get chocolate if you follow the general.

It started out with a wedding. Really, it did. The son of a renowned Kurdish leader was getting married in the reputably beautiful city of Suleimaniyah in Iraqi Kurdistan. It was an embattled area near the border with Iran. Geographically, it counts as Northern Iraq.

It was December 2003, and the Kurdish leader was a favourite of the US occupiers. A charming politician with an even more charming British-educated son.

The son and I became fast phone pals. He was always accessible to confirm a story or discuss questionable information. And he readily shared more details than their press office.

So, this up-and-coming statesman was getting married—and one of our senior correspondents was invited to the nuptials. She wanted to go—but our Baghdad bureau was incredibly busy, and the usual roster of reporters was incomplete. Also, Suleimaniyah was at least a five-hour-drive, and a trip over would've meant a convoy of vehicles and a security escort. Taking these resources away from the team in Baghdad. All things considered, the newsdesk was not leaning towards letting this correspondent leave the Iraqi capital just for a wedding.

But correspondents don't get to where they are without being resourceful. And what started out as destination wedding became a legitimate hunt for news.

'We haven't been up north recently … ' she contended, 'and with the latest attacks, there's talk that terrorist groups with ties to Iran are hiding in Kurdish territory. We should investigate.'

She had a point. I heard the whole discussion and any newsdesk knows there's no arguing with determined reporters. So, she was given the go-ahead.

'And I'd like Marga to come as my producer.'

What?!

That was how she closed her argument.

And that was the end of that.

Onward

So, off we went to Suleimaniyah for the weekend with a cameraman, a security adviser, and Odai—who didn't speak Kurdish but begged to come along for the ride. I was glad for the extra hand and the company.

We packed two massive vehicles with our gear, our bags, loads of local food, and two kettles (one with coffee and one with tea). Behind the wheel of each vehicle would be our most experienced drivers.

It had all the makings of a cruisy assignment—except I got lobbed with it less than forty-eight hours before we were set to leave, which meant barely any time to set up stories.

Iraqis were notoriously flaky when it came to planning and schedules, but I learnt very quickly that they had nothing on the Kurds!

Bar the groom and his family, who obviously had better things to do that weekend than help us journos, the correspondent had one other contact up in Suleimaniyah, aka Suli. But said contact was ridiculously difficult to pin down. I spent the entire day before the trip trying to arrange with her for a local driver and a Kurdish translator, as well as asking for her help in booking us rooms. It was near impossible to call any landlines outside of Baghdad and even more difficult to try to reach people on satellite phones.

By the time we hit the road, the only thing we had locked down was the name of a hotel.

The Drive

Fortunately, this was uneventful. Sort of. About three hours in, we got stuck at a roadblock because Peshmerga—Kurdish fighters transformed into the Iraqi Civil Defence Corps—had discovered an improvised explosive device (IED) and were trying to get it defused.

Needing to get to Suli in time for the evening wedding, our ever-resourceful reporter got us through the barricade and back on our way by chit-chatting and giving the soldiers the latest edition of *Marie Claire* magazine! Bye-bye to a pouting Angelina Jolie and the latest in bedroom etiquette.

I must say, the much-touted Kurdish landscape didn't disappoint. It was indeed quite pretty—and very distinct from Baghdad.

For one thing, it wasn't flat. The desert terrain suddenly raised itself into hills and mountains. The scenery and foliage changed from dirt and date palms to oil fields, then to lush green peaks and rows of pine trees. Pine trees! It was stunning. Like suddenly being in an entirely different country. Well, as far as the Kurds are concerned, we were in a different country—theirs. Technically, the autonomous region of Kurdistan.

I remember being grateful that I didn't need the restroom—there were no roadside service stations anywhere on that five-hour trek.

The Arrival

The first thing that struck me once we got to Suli proper was that there were lights. Wow. After months of relying on generators further south, here there was electricity. And the traffic lights worked. Not only did they work, but people followed them. What a change from the mess of Baghdad streets.

Our first stop was the grand Palace Hotel right in the centre of town. Compared to our run-down, freshly bombed hotel in Baghdad—this was indeed a palace! Sparkling—clean—brightly lit lobby. Colourful flowers in vases and smiling attendants. All of whom seemed to speak English.

I was so looking forward to a shower and a bed. But it turned out that the hotel was fully booked for the big wedding, and our contact—who was meant to meet us there—instead had to get us rooms in 'another nice place just down the street'. That's the message we were given by her assistant as soon as we arrived.

As for the translator and driver that the contact was also meant to arrange, according to her assistant, that had escaped her attention. Great.

When I tried the contact's phone, it seemed she'd 'gone out' and left the device with her twelve-year-old daughter.

So, it was 5 p.m. and we were finally in Suli—without rooms at the hotel, no translator nor local driver. Of course.

The Wedding

We were nowhere near it. After changing into a dress in the Palace Hotel's loo—our correspondent left with an official convoy to the 'undisclosed' wedding location.

They promised to get her back to us somehow later in the evening.

There was not much else we could do about it.

So, off we went to 'another nice place just down the street'.

The New 'Hotel'

... was revolting. It also wasn't 'down the street'—more like just-kinda-sorta-still-barely-within-the-town. There were dead bugs on the beds—big ones, not tiny little mites—and grime all over the bathrooms. The poor security adviser ended up with a room that stank of sewage because the drains backed up into his shower. For real. You couldn't walk past his shut door without wanting to vomit. It was dreadful.

Oh, and I must mention that this hotel was infamous for people throwing themselves off its roof.

New Arrangements

Nope. We could not move to another hotel. With the wedding, there were no more available rooms in town. They barely had enough to spare in this place.

But there was no point in dwelling on the state of our dwellings—so, I just carried on trying to set up a story for us to film in the morning. We only had that one day to come up with a viable news report before needing to head back down to Baghdad.

With the help of our security adviser—the only one of our crew who had been in Suli before—we finally found a local driver and a Kurdish translator. They came to meet us that same evening so we could make plans and iron out a schedule.

I also managed to find an independent social worker who agreed to take us to a remote village that had been victimised by the terror group we wanted to investigate.

Despite the odds, we chugged away, and things were beginning to fall into place.

After all these instantaneous meetings, I proudly left a note with the reporter's room key at 'reception', letting her know the plans for the morning.

Then, finally, the crew and I could sit down to a cold, tasteless meal and call it a night.

New *New* Arrangements

My room phone rang at one in the morning. I know the time because I was in deep sleep and reached for my watch immediately after the loud *krrrrringing* woke me up.

It was the reporter.

'I want to talk about the morning.'

Sure. How was the wedding?

'Great. Lovely. Had a wonderful time.'

That's nice. You just back?

'Yes.'

Room ok?

'Fine. Not too shabby.' (I found out later she was just being polite.)

Cool.

I then launched into my spiel about the morning's plans. Blah-blah-blah-blah-blah. Driver and translator will be here by 8 a.m. Aid worker in by 9 a.m. We drive to this village an hour and a half away, should be there by 10.30. We scout for an interviewee and possible stories ...

She let me go on and on, and then ...

'Great. That's great. But ...'

But?

'... I was sitting next to the general at dinner ...'

Of course.

'Great guy. Love him.'

Ok.

'So, I was talking to the general ...'

Uh-huh ... I had no idea where this was going.

'Apparently, tomorrow he is leaving at 9 a.m. from the Kurdish base to meet with former Iraqi officers ...'

Uh-huh ...?

'And then, he's going to this model-village or something that the US military helped build. Where Kurds and Arabs are going to be living together ...'

Uh-huh.

'After that, he's off to a coalition base to meet with some top-level officers about a new anti-insurgency plan ...'

And then?

'And then'—I could hear in her voice the huge grin she must've had on her face—'and then, he caps it all off by meeting with tribal and religious leaders in ... [dramatic pause] ... Hatra!'

Right.

'Hatra!' she repeated, as if I hadn't heard her.

Ok. I admit—I had absolutely no idea where or what Hatra was, much less why she seemed so excited about it.

Right—I said, still failing to get her point.

'So, what do you think?!'

About what?

'The plans for the morning!'

Huh? Didn't I just go over that? Well, at 8 a.m. the driver and the translator are coming over ...

I began my spiel again.

'No-no-no.'

What?

'Hatra! Retired Iraqi generals ... model-village ... Hatra!'

Ok. I still didn't get it, so I had to ask her to spell out exactly what she was trying to tell me.

'The American general invited us along!'

Huh?!

'Surely we can put together a story out of all that?'

Out of what?!

'Retired generals—model-village—HATRA!'

'Oh. *HATRA*! I get it.'

Honestly, I had no clue what we were talking about anymore, but in her excitement, she just kept repeating the general's itinerary.

'Nine a.m. tomorrow. From the Kurdish military base in the mountains, and he says we can ride with them on the Black Hawks!'

At this point, I woke up properly. Black Hawks?! You mean the choppers that had been involved in multiple crashes lately? One being shot down, and two others colliding in mid-air because they were ... well, *shot at* in inclement weather?!

Of course, I didn't say this out loud—but I was thinking it. Lord, we covered those stories just a few days ago out of Baghdad.

'Isn't this cool?!'

Silence.

'So? Hatra! What are your thoughts? We must be able to come up with a worthwhile, coherent story from all of that? Right? Hatra!'

My thoughts? A bed without bugs? Some sleep? Silence?

But I didn't say that out loud either.

What I did say was: 'Well, we can look at it as a grassroots attempt by the US-led coalition to pull together the disparate strings of this fractured society. You've got everything there— the disgruntled, disillusioned military, inflamed religious leaders, discordant ethnic groups—and all culminating against the dramatic backdrop of Hatra.' (At this point she had let on that Hatra was an ancient ruin going back to like BCE days—one of the foundations of Iraqi society and all that.) If anything, at least the pictures would be great. So yeah, heck, of course we could pull a story together. Even my sleepy 1 a.m. brain could see that.

'Fantastic! I knew I could count on you. You'll get the crew up? We should have a planning meeting now so everyone's on the same page before the morning. See you all in my room.'

Right. Of course.

So, at nearly 1.30 a.m.—and I didn't even bother to change out of my pyjamas—I dragged myself over to the videographer's room and banged on his door. Instead of rousing him, I earned the attention of two drunk Americans across the hall who thought I might be coerced into joining their little party.

I managed to get away from the revellers and head towards the poor security adviser trying to slumber amid the stench of sewage.

The crew thought I was out of my head and couldn't understand my gibberish about 'the general'—tomorrow—Black Hawks—Hatra.

The reporter laid it out to them plainly when we got to her room. And with sleep still in their eyes, the chaps just nodded silently. *Sure. Great. Hatra.* It was all they could muster.

Cutting It

To make a long story shorter, I had to ring the Kurdish translator that same night to cancel (yes, at nearly 2 a.m.) as it was decided he wouldn't be needed on a jaunt with the US general.

The local driver had to be rung too, since we needed him to come earlier to lead us up the mountains to this Kurdish air base to catch the Black Hawks before they took off at 9 a.m. (This was still a few years before smartphones and live map apps.)

The woman aid worker I rang at a more decent time later that morning.

After a few more hours' uncomfortable sleep with my dead bugs, the vehicles were packed again as we'd hoped to bring some of our broadcast equipment on the choppers with us.

The Rest of the Day

We were at the air base exactly on time, catching a rather surprised American general mid-preparation for his departure. He was visibly amazed we'd taken him up on what now appeared to be just a polite offer.

It was only when we were briefed that we realized the choppers were not returning to Suli at the end of the day—we would be let off in Mosul, on the opposite side of northern Iraq. More than 250 kilometres away. But of course.

After a quick discussion, it was decided that the reporter, cameraman, Odai, and I would get on the choppers, while the security adviser would head to Mosul with our two vehicles and all our gear. To hopefully meet us there by nightfall. Because of weight restrictions, we were only allowed to bring the camera— so, there went the option to report live from any of the stops along the journey.

It was also pouring rain. And I must say that getting a ride in a Black Hawk seemed even less fun in a storm.

Aside from all that, one of our vehicles stalled the minute we took off—but we weren't aware of this until much, much later.

So, yes, a glorious start to the day all around.

Seriously

It was. A glorious day. After all the palaver, it was worth it.

Odai and I were half petrified going up in the chopper the first time. He kept looking at me, wide-eyed, muttering the title of a Hollywood film under his breath: '*Black Hawk Down! Black Hawk Down!*' It was not funny.

But we quickly put aside those movie scenes when we saw the breath-taking Kurdish mountains from on high. What a sight! Such remarkable terrain. I will try but know that words fail to describe it. The landscape was a combination of surprisingly bright green patches on muted red ranges. With glossy, glass-like rivers of burnt umber winding through its curves.

And then, it began to snow!

Bless him, Odai was as excited as a three-year-old receiving his first bicycle. It was the first time he'd seen such snowfall. His expression alone made the trip up in the chopper worth it. He took the black-market digital camera Duraid got me and took picture after picture out the window. Each view only got better than the last.

We spent the entire day landing in places we didn't even know existed. We didn't even know their names.

I tried to ring the Baghdad bureau as often as I could to let them know how we were getting on, but that proved difficult when I couldn't even tell them where we were.

Unbeknown to me at the time, the security convoy we'd left in Suli was having troubles of their own—and weren't sure they would make it to Mosul by nightfall.

Anyway, by 5 p.m., after:

1. a rather extraordinary, emotional meeting with Saddam's former generals, (I couldn't hear what was said, but there was a lot of impassioned gesturing, back patting and hand-clasping, and I think I even recall some tears),
2. an incredibly wet visit to a muddy cluster of cinderblock structures that we were later told was Dugirdkan, meaning 'between two mountains', a rebuilt village that was to serve as a model that Arabs and Kurds (historical enemies) could live side by side, and where the US general—in full battle gear—was welcomed by villagers in their finery, waiting in the rain for him to cut a pink ribbon and inaugurate the village, and, lastly—
3. an interesting briefing at a US camp where we listened in, off the record, as officers planned their next operation against 'insurgents'—(can you believe they serve tea and cakes at these things?)—we landed in …

Hatra

In a word: astonishing. A UNESCO World Heritage site, this massive, fortified city was deemed an impressive and well-preserved example of ancient empires. It was the capital of the first Arab kingdom. A centre of trade and religion. Its rulers' language was Aramaic, and because of all its temples, it was once known as 'House of God'.

Over two-thousand years old, what remained of Hatra resembled Ancient Greece. Except in colour. Instead of white marble and limestone, it was all red sand and yellow boulders. And when we got there, everything was dressed in a stunning crimson sunset. Can you imagine?

While the reporter and the cameraman continued filming, schmoozing with the general and meeting the tribal leaders, Odai and I were able to explore the ruins like tourists. Just the two of us walking around with our mouths hanging open. And I mean—hanging open. With my wee camera, we took turns snapping golden photos in the magical afternoon light.

Built in a circle—as per military tradition—Hatra had inner and outer walls that helped it withstand attacks by the Roman Empire. But the city was eventually abandoned in the third century CE after being overrun by Persia. Its historical remains survived until it was vandalized and further destroyed by the Islamic State in 2015. When this news came out, I was evermore grateful we didn't stick to our original coverage plans in 2003.

'See? Didn't I tell you it would be worth it?' the reporter said to me then when we got to Hatra. She was as thrilled as a child receiving a truckload of birthday presents.

I did admit to her that she was right.

We got wonderful images, and our videographer—being the fantastic shooter that he is—even caught on camera the tribal leaders' befuddlement as a US soldier rather insensitively regaled them with a rendition of 'God Bless the U-S-A!' It spoke so much to how relations between them were going.

Thank goodness the tribal elders couldn't speak English!

Well, as the reporter put it, at least the Americans were *trying*.

Back to Base

The team we'd left in Suli did eventually make it to Mosul with our bags and our vehicles, and after a restful night in a decent hotel—the Nineveh Palace this time—we headed home. Back to Baghdad, I mean.

We cut a nice piece—with great exclusive pictures—and got pats on the back for making it all work.

The following Monday morning, a very chirpy, nearly conspiratorial reporter came by my workspace and put something down on my desk.

'For you,' she winked, before walking away. It was a gift of solidarity from her to me. A small golden ball.

It was a much-coveted piece of Ferrero Rocher chocolate. A luxurious treat that had become for us a symbol of hope and life beyond a warzone.

The Final Word

At every point on this assignment, challenges cropped up that could've left us feeling that things were going to pot. But the entire trip to Suli taught me to see things differently. And that to stay sane and effective as a journalist, there is one thing you must master—which also turned out to be a most important life lesson—**no matter the obstacle that appears, you can always pivot.**

Jerusalem

IT DOESN'T MEAN YOU'RE LOST JUST BECAUSE YOU DON'T KNOW WHERE YOU ARE.

Usually, when you take a holiday tour, you know where you're headed and what you're in for. Presumably because you made the choice to begin with, after careful planning. But once in a while, that may not be how it transpires.

Meeting Mohammed

I wasn't planning to take a sight-seeing tour of the Holy Land in 2015, but when Al Jazeera sent me on assignment, it came as a bonus. A remarkable if troubled destination, it gets millions of visitors every year—despite long-standing religious and political tension among its inhabitants.

Sacred to multiple faiths, the Holy Land includes Palestinian territories, Jordan, parts of Lebanon and Syria, and of course, modern-day Israel. The Jewish state and its Muslim neighbours remain at odds (to put it mildly). Their ongoing struggle for sovereignty and dominance usually headlines the news from the region. Which is why I was in the Palestinian territory of Gaza.

When my assignment ended, a man called Mohammed was sent to pick me up at the border between Gaza and Israel. He was to take me back to Jerusalem for my flight out the next morning.

It was a two-hour drive, in usual traffic. The sun was shining, the weather was mild, and he seemed in no hurry.

Mohammed could barely speak English—nor did he know much about Judaism or Christianity—but he very kindly offered me a tour of some sights along the way. That much I understood from his gestures. He motioned that there were things I should see of the Holy Land other than what was on the news. 'Important place,' he would utter at every stop, 'important to see.'

I had been there before—but saw little other than the most troubled spots. So, I agreed to Mohammed's kind offer. I don't know what it was exactly that made me do so, but I trusted my gut—which trusted Mohammed.

It was a rather silent journey in his rented taxi. He drove from one location to the next without saying a word. Then, he'd stop, point at a structure, and gesture for me to go see it. I did as he suggested at every turn.

I must confess that at the time, I didn't know for sure where I was or what exactly I was looking at. But I went with it.

Lost Lamb

At one point, I was shocked to be the only person at what I thought was Christ's burial site—only to find out later that although I *did* have it right, there was a spot further down considered more important (and therefore, more crowded). Calvary, the place of Christ's crucifixion. I had no idea that's what it was when I was there.

Instead of an open hill, the crucifixion site had been enclosed in a church, ornately decorated and gilded. There were chandeliers, candelabras, and icons. Slabs of rich marble, carpets of flowers, and masterful paintings. It was full of dimly lit chambers opening to other chambers, and the whole place was packed with visitors.

In many of our 'tour' stops, I followed the crowd like a lamb, noticing where their attention went without understanding why. I wanted to make sure I took everything in. Which wasn't hard to do in a land that inherently inspired reverence.

I also got into queues not knowing where they led. But I joined them anyway and snapped tons of photos, planning to later look them up online.

Thank goodness I did so. I discovered that thanks to Mohammed I got to see the Church of the Nativity, believed to hold the site of Christ's birth.

Inside the church, there's a small door in the main nave that leads to a narrow, winding stairwell, which descends to an underground grotto otherwise known as the Christmas Cave. Small but encased in decorative details. The walls were stone but festooned with tapestries and lamps. Set in the floor was a silver star, meant to mark the place where Christ was born. There was a marble altar behind it and a Latin inscription.

This Church is on the Palestinian West Bank and cared for by three different Christian denominations. Yes, the situation is as complex as it sounds.

Communion

After much warfare and political conflict involving Russia, Turkey, and most of Europe, an agreement over the Church of the Nativity was reached in the late 1800s. The Greek Orthodox Church was made responsible for the main basilica. The Armenian Apostolic Church oversees the northern transept, while the Roman Catholics have the southern transept. It's basically custody sharing in an amicable divorce. And in the one structure, each denomination has its chapels, alcoves, and its faithful.

The site is bannered as 'the oldest major church in the Holy Land, and the grotto is the oldest, continuously used place of worship in Christianity.'

Again, I did not know this at the time, but Google's been a great help since. And despite not fully understanding the location or its background, I could appreciate it was a beautiful church that evoked admiration and a sense of the divine.

I also got to see the Garden at Gethsemane, the Church of Mary Magdalene, and other sites sacred to Christians.

Mohammed and the Mount

Then, Mohammed brought me to a place with the best view of Old Jerusalem: Mount of Olives. A historical ridge just east of the Walled City. It offered an amazing panorama of the hallowed ancient sprawl at the heart of three religions: Judaism, Islam, and Christianity.

Rising above all the sand-coloured limestone, the Dome of the Rock—with its golden crown—shone brilliantly in the desert sun.

But you couldn't see Old Jerusalem without also taking in what was at the base of the Mount—where there once were olive groves lay the oldest and most important Jewish cemetery. Thousands upon thousands of graves like miniature cities. A constant reminder of Jerusalem's sacred and complex history— and the many people, Jewish and otherwise, who have died for its cause.

Though its conflicts remain unresolved and it is still a place of tensions, that one bright day, it also showed that it held the space for peace.

Chukran, Mohammed

If not for Mohammed, I would have left the Holy Land only seeing its open wounds. But now, my last memory is of the wonderful

Muslim man who didn't feel the need to figure out who I was so he could put me in a box and manage our interaction, and instead drove me to the most sacred sites of Islam and Christianity and showed me the wonders of the Jewish homeland.

I'll forever be buoyed by the shared humanity I witnessed there. When people treated each other as kin despite the manmade divisions of institutionalized religion and politics.

Faith and hope have always transcended borders. And it's surprising what you might see when you **have no expectations**.

Gaza

WHEN ALL ELSE FAILS, THERE'S DISCO.

In March 2004, Sheikh Ahmed Yassin was killed by an Israeli airstrike outside his home in Gaza, a beautiful strip of Palestinian land fronting the Mediterranean Sea. On one side, Gaza is bordered by Egypt, and the rest of it is walled in with access controlled by the Jewish state.

Sheikh Yassin was the founder and spiritual leader of Hamas, a militant group fighting since the 1980s for the creation of a Palestinian state in place of Israel.

Hamas—which means 'zeal' in Arabic and 'violence' in Hebrew—was then (and remains) on an international list of terror organizations. Serious retaliation was expected for the killing of their founder.

I had just come out of a long, difficult tour of duty in Iraq for CNN and was meant to be flying home to London from Amman in Jordan. I got a call from the newsdesk about the Gaza assassination while in the departure area. That was the only time I ever withdrew from a flight—and had to be escorted back out of an airport. All the while, I had to listen to the airline's ground officer go on about the evils of the media.

A camerawoman—also fresh out of Baghdad—was waiting for me in Amman so we could set off together to Israel. She had long worked with the assigned correspondent, and they were known as a dynamic duo. I would be along as their producer, happy just to work alongside them again after our first encounter, in person, in Iraq.

The Gaza airport was destroyed by Israel in 2001, and the only access to the Strip was by land. So, we were driven across the Jordanian desert and through the border with Israel, where the correspondent met us.

After a stop in Jerusalem to sort out permits and pick up protective gear, we could then head on to Gaza.

It was my first time in either place.

I'm often asked if I was ever scared to go into areas of conflict—or rather, *conflicted* areas. Truth is, every time I was given such assignments, it was so rushed there wasn't time to think about it. And when on location, you're too busy working to have space for fear. Or little else. It's a bit like being wounded or suffering a trauma. You don't feel anything initially because your nerves are in shock.

The pain comes later.

In a way, that helped with the work—to not consider your feelings. To not think about your-*self*.

When I was sent to Gaza that first time, I wasn't *thinking* at all. As mentioned, we were just out of a difficult tour of duty in Baghdad. One like no other. Our colleagues—our friends—were killed in an ambush, and I think my emotions were numb. As such, I accepted the Gaza assignment without question.

I have never regretted it.

Firstly, it was a chance to work with one of CNN's best teams—a camerawoman and correspondent who are among the pantheon of greats. They were experienced and effective. Old hands at covering the complex Palestinian conflict. A *huge* bonus for a first timer like me to go into such a complicated story with them. I learnt so much from this team, not just about how to handle a difficult story—but also how to deal with the traumatized people who inhabit it.

Frankly, those two were a well-oiled machine and didn't really need me on that assignment—but it was among the privileges of my career that I was with them.

Borderline

We arrived at Erez Pass very late that night. And due to unforeseen circumstances—a rocket attack just minutes earlier—there were only a handful of people working.

No, the drive didn't account for the length of our trip from Amman, which we'd left even before noon. It was the red tape and security procedures that delayed us. It was only two hours from the Jordanian capital to the border, but we were held there for nearly five by the Israelis. As I would later discover, that was the easy part!

Once we were allowed into Israel, the drive to Jerusalem was under an hour. From there—after completing the necessary errands—it would be another hour's drive to Erez Pass, the entry point to Gaza.

Operated by the Israeli military, Erez Pass is one of the most fortified border crossings in the world—meant to protect the country from those it sees as its greatest enemies. Its neighbours. I wrote in my notebook then that it made Baghdad—with its heavily armed guards, endless concrete barricades, and thick, thick blast walls—seem like Disneyland.

In 2004, there were 1.2 million Palestinians living in the enclave of Gaza, and everything they had access to was controlled by someone else. They couldn't even go to their beautiful beaches without permission from the Israelis. And when they did, how far into the water they could go was also limited. Majority of Gazan households lacked basic services and relied on aid. They were also at the level of subsistence poverty. (Not much has changed in the two decades since.)

In 2004, Gaza was as devastated as any warzone. Albeit the destruction was more concentrated because of its size. A 365-square-kilometre sitting duck, enclosed by the world's most armed country.

Daily life went on as *normally* as possible, given that many of its streets were nothing but rubble and the structures left standing—pockmarked with bullet holes—were constant reminders of the uncertainty of their existence. Shelling could begin again at any time, and everyone knew it. Both sides of this conflict were fighting for their survival.

I remember sitting for a meal outside the place we were staying. It was by the beach and had a view of the sea. As dusk fell, a soothing wind rustled and gentle waves crashed reassuringly on the shore. Soft lights on distant fishing boats began to reach us, and it felt to me like sitting along the Costa Brava in Spain.

Until these sharp red pin lights zipped across the newly pitch-black sky.

For a moment, naïve me thought they might have been shooting stars—then I heard a whoosh so potent it felt like a cosmic movement.

'Israeli gunships,' another journalist said. Heavily armed aircraft most likely obtained from the US. 'A nightly visit'—the journo went on—'you can count them like sheep, but they won't put you to sleep.'

Then, a succession of flares was fired from the war planes. Seconds later, a flash of white in the distance, followed by a resounding boom. There were several more within seconds.

Shooting stars, indeed.

The illusion of our lovely dinner—which almost had me forgetting where we were—was shattered. A brazen reminder that life in Gaza was dictated by fear and insecurity.

Which is beyond evident the moment you reach Erez Pass.

Let me describe it for you: the pedestrian/cargo crossing in Gaza's northern end was made up of cold, large, concrete buildings and labyrinthine caged corridors topped by heat-trapping, corrugated metal roofing. The night we got there, I couldn't have been faulted for thinking the narrow passages were within a structure—there were no lights on, and the moon barely cut a sliver in the darkness.

It was a civilian crossing open only to residents, aid workers, and those who obtained special permission. The people who used it went predominantly in one direction—out.

When we arrived that night, the crossing was near closing. I was told there were usually Palestinians working as porters to help you get your bags through and to the other side. But after the earlier rocket attack, none of them were there.

Our team of three had to move not only our personal bags through the lengthy corridor but all twenty cases of broadcast equipment. No help. No baggage cart. Just the reporter, the shooter, and me. Like pack mules. (I guess I served a wee tiny purpose after all!)

For a fit, healthy person, that trek could take some fifteen to twenty minutes. Imagine that with twenty-plus heavy cases.

At one point, we bumped into another news team on their way out, and they were kind enough to loan us their foldable two-wheel trolley.

It was nearly midnight when we got to our workspace in Gaza. Just in time for the correspondent's first live. (That's when a journalist on location delivers his report to you *live* on camera into the news program.)

Our day had started at dawn, and we didn't get to bed until around three the next morning. Par for the course when you work in news.

The Mourning After

I didn't know how we would manage again to rise early and get through another full day's work—but let me tell you, ten cups of coffee help. Do note that a full day's work by twenty-four-hour TV news standards is nowhere near an eight-hour day. Especially not when you're out on assignment.

Once we got through the morning live shots, we were able to finally move around Gaza and newsgather—which is when journalists go around filming elements for their day's story. Recording interviews, general scenes, etcetera.

So, the morning after our entry to Gaza, we headed to the mourning sites for Sheikh Yassin.

I learnt all about how Muslims mourn while in Iraq. It was happening there all too frequently. Burial within twenty-four hours and a three-day wake, as it was for Yasser and Duraid. We went to their homes and sat to condole with their families, who were more accommodating than traditional—i.e., they let us women sit with the men. If slightly off to the side.

In Baghdad, more and more mourning tents went up every day, anywhere there was a large open space. One tent for the men, who huddled together, shaking hands, and one—somewhere else—for the women. It struck me that they mourned separately. You would think that if anything would bring people together it would be death, but again, that was naïve of me.

Where were we? Oh yes, the mourning for Sheikh Yassin.

It was a very hot morning. We'd gone from a freezing night to this blistering day. The extremes of desert weather. In the centre of town—in the sweltering heat—a massive green tent had been set up for the men in an open-air stadium. There were already hundreds of mourners there before midday. The crowd filled the playing field and stretched out almost to the street. It was a sea of Hamas green. There were green flags everywhere, and black and green bands on everyone's heads. Green banners were stretched across every possible surface. And a loudspeaker blared continuous battle speeches and praises for Sheikh Yassin and his martyrdom.

This was my introduction to Hamas.

What can I tell you about the men's grieving area? It was loud. Angry. And a tad aggressive. It felt like those in attendance were driven by duty. A responsibility to participate. To see and be seen. Their grief felt vicious. It left me cold.

Our shooter and I were the only women there, and soon we were accosted by an unruly pack of boisterous male children. They were around us like flies on rotten fruit, making filming nearly impossible. It was not a pleasant experience.

A few hours later, we went to see the assassination site, which was right outside the victim's home. Supposedly a rundown, slum area. But from what I saw, it was no more rundown or ravaged than any other part of Gaza.

We stepped out of a van and soon found ourselves among a steady stream of women. Dressed shapelessly in black from head to toe. Aside from the abaya, many of them also had their faces fully covered. If you looked close enough though, you might see their eyes. And with only that to distinguish them, the clear emotion was so striking it threatened to drown anyone who dared a glance.

Belying their evident sorrow, the women were warm and welcoming. And as the cameraperson and I were also female, they brought us to join the mourners in the widow's tent. It was set up right behind the home and it was packed.

Immediately, we were offered a meal and invited to stay. Many of the women there could speak English, and they were eloquent, intelligent, and interested.

We were the only news team present and they allowed us to film, a little fascinated by the sight of a female TV crew. (Oh, what networks miss at times when they only send out men.)

'Can I please tell you how I feel?' many of them asked, huddling around. At first, they touched us gently as if we would break, then they grabbed our arms and held our hands like lifelines. Impressing upon us how glad they were we were there. 'Please, please would you listen to my story?'

Their stories nearly all began the same: 'The Israelis killed my brother … My husband was shot … my father and my sons … they bombed my neighbourhood … they stopped us from working … they took our homes … why? Why? Why does the world just watch and let them do this? Do you hate us that much? *Why* do you hate us? Arab, American, Israeli—are we not all the same? When will this end?'

Over and over, we were asked these questions.

It broke our hearts.

Mothers held their babies tight to their bosoms. Children sat motionless next to the adults, all staring at us, wide-eyed, waiting for answers.

My chest began to hurt. I needed air.

And that's when I met Ruba. A twenty-five-year-old English teacher who was fifth in a family of eight. She slowly led me away from the crowd growing around us and offered to help. 'I can introduce you to the Sheikh's widow and translate for you, if you want.'

In her grey abaya, Ruba was a blessing.

I followed her to the Sheikh's home, and we waited for his widow to be done with her prayers.

Ruba was intrigued by my face and asked where I was from. Curious to know everything I could tell her. Turned out, she knew about the Philippines and Christianity, and had positive impressions of both.

Meanwhile, the camerawoman was surrounded by a bevy of observers. She was American, and they all wanted to know what she had to say. Did the US really hate them so to keep arming Israel? Did the whole world just want to see them dead?

There was no anger or hatred behind any of their questions, just a desire to understand why things were as they were. Both she and I were shaken by the experience. It was more profound than either of us had expected.

It was like being taken into a warm but painful hug and reminded yet again that we're all connected. We're all just people trying to get by in the madness. Wanting to love, conquer our fears, and fulfil our needs.

Our differences? Well, everything at the roll of a die.

A few days later, a fourteen-year-old Palestinian boy was caught trying to get into Israel with an explosive belt strapped around him. He said he wanted to die and go to heaven. His mother thought he was in school. What kind of a life is it when your childhood dream is to go to your grave?

In Gaza, people said they often felt like the living dead.

Colours

Which is not to say it was a lifeless spot.

Besides the green of Hamas, like any other town, there was a rainbow of hues.

In the central souk—where we spent time to get a feel of the city's pulse—the old mosque's pale white walls burst into colour at the winding alleys of the market. Stalls full of assorted candies, vegetables, and meats. Pastries and sweet breads, toys and pottery.

There were shoes, too, and clothing. Plus, of course, endless vibrant rows of spices and herbs.

There was also so much gold that the souk seemed to glow from within.

Men, just metres away from each other, called out their special wares and lowest prices. Juice vendors walked around with intricately engraved canisters slung to their backs, ready to pour a thirsty pundit a cold glass of carob juice. With bright pink and purple roses tied to the top of their containers—and a waistband holding eight or so clinking glasses—you could spot them a mile away.

And then, there was the smell. Oh, the rich, complex scents that wove the scene together: the incense; the salted fish; the dirty water, stagnant on the uncleaned roads; the perfume; the sweaty children. A wondrous sensory carpet.

We sat in a tea shop where the fragrant aromas of the *narghiles* tiptoed into your nostrils and caressed you like a lover just before sleep. Men sat low on the yellow-tiled floor blowing into water pipes and filling the tiny room with smoke. You could get lost in it.

And at the end of the day, Gaza hosted the most fragile sunsets. Thin slivers of platinum sun cut through gossamer clouds, creating a filigree fan that stretched down to lay light gold flecks on the weary Mediterranean Sea. It was breath-taking. And eternal.

Then, night fell. Suddenly. Solidly. Leaving nothing of the gentle touch of dusk. Often, there'd be no power, while over-head—all around—the call to prayer resounded from mosques across the Strip. Muezzins crying out into the darkness, filling the heavy air with anguish. There was such torment in the chorus of voices echoing through the opaque evenings.

The sights and sounds of Gaza.

They could suffocate you with their weight.

Another Day

It was a whirlwind—endless—week full of revelations. A masterclass in human strength and frailty. I never in a million years thought I would get to Gaza—and every day, I am grateful that I did.

We worked around the clock and were exhausted, but nothing felt wearier than my soul. Which also expanded in unexpected ways. I was grateful—and I took it all in.

On our last evening, I was up on the roof of our office building, looking forward to watching a final sunset. But it didn't come. Instead, a heavy fog rolled in from the sea—rapidly hiding the battered city beneath my tenth-floor perch. A thick veil, an all-consuming gauze of grey and white. Nothing was visible on the street below. It was as if the air itself had been siphoned away.

Then, on cue—needling through the dense haze—the call to evening prayer began. Like a frequent interloper descending on a flying carpet, to stir the turbulent darkness once more.

That final afternoon, I watched a fog roll in over Gaza, roughly hiding what it could not erase—the wounds that would still be there in the morning light.

Parachute and Chocolate

Journalists often speak of 'parachuting' into a 'story'—we got dropped in then pulled out. Rapidly digesting and reducing people's realities to less than two minutes of TV. That is the privilege of the job, and its cruelty.

Those we 'cover' don't have the luxury of 'escape' and must deal with the truths of their existence once the news cameras are gone.

After this time in the Middle East, I learnt what it was like to carry the weight of people's stories—and the role that journalists play in bearing witness. Our job was to serve as a funnel, a conduit, and in so doing, hopefully remind viewers across the world that we're all the same. To elicit even a smidgen of empathy for those who might *seem* different to you.

Years later, back in Gaza as a correspondent, the local producer insisted on taking me out 'for a treat' at the end of a workday. After winding through the city's rubble—Gaza's never quite had the chance to rebuild—we found ourselves at a corner store packed with people and balloons. There were buntings, flowers, and confetti. And the walls were covered with candy.

It was the opening of a sweetshop. And there were confections—so I was told—that came all the way from Syria and Lebanon. No easy feat under a blockade.

There were so many smiling children in that store. And indeed, it was a treat to see the shape of life's simple joys amid its many hardships.

Exit

The first time I saw the actual barbarity of Erez Pass was in 2004, at the end of our Sheikh Yassin assignment. We left Gaza after an intense and sleepless week, to head back to Jerusalem and onward flights to our home bureaux.

After we were driven to the border, the team and I went down the same, long, cold corridor that brought us into Palestine—but in the harsh light of day, I could finally see what it looked like. This was the path regularly taken by thousands of Palestinians when they needed to get to Israel. Most of them working at a nearby industrial zone. But even after being practically strip searched daily, there was no guarantee they'd be let through.

I remember wishing for the darkness of night to spare me the sight of their degradation.

In the sun, what was known as 'No Man's Land' was—in a word—shocking. To say the least. Inhuman, really.

The walkway was strewn with rubbish, and the only gaps between the concrete walls and the sheet metal roof were just over a metre above our heads, where a wire mesh siphoned in light and air.

The walls themselves were covered in graffiti. Nearly from end to end.

'This is no way to live,' translated our Arabic-speaking correspondent.

'Are we no better than animals?' he read out another one.

On and on the same sentiment on the Erez Pass walls. It was depressing.

Near the end of the corridor, we were stopped by fortified iron gates and locked floor-to-ceiling turnstiles. Passage was controlled by heavily armed Israeli soldiers at the far end, their offices and watch posts elevated from the ground. A safety precaution after several suicide bomb attacks by Palestinian militants.

All around us—there were mothers with their young children waiting to be let through, and businesspeople in suits rushing to make their appointments in Israeli cities.

The queue wasn't moving, and no one was being allowed passage. No explanation. It just wasn't time yet. That's exactly what we were told. 'It's not time yet,' and the world was put on pause.

So, we joined the queue … and waited. I looked around and was struck by how much this resembled a detention camp. We were all powerless, in an enclosure manned by folks with guns.

We waited some more.

The businessmen waited. The mothers and their children— waited. In the cramped space. In the heat. At that point, some of the people in the queue had been waiting for more than two hours.

I quickly learnt that at Erez, you waited until the Israeli soldiers on the other end decided you could come forward. And there were no set guidelines for that.

So, we kept waiting. With all the others needing to get through.

Such a crush of people was common on the Palestinian side of Erez Pass—and I found out that a few months earlier, not only had someone died of suffocation while waiting, but twenty-five other Palestinians were injured in the queue by Israeli soldiers firing in their direction.

It's a good thing I didn't know this at the time or what happened next may not have happened.

People's Playlist

After about an hour, our reporter called out to the Israeli soldiers: 'News! TV! We need to get through—please!'

TV? It got their attention. They called him forward. He exchanged a few words with them, then was told to get back in line and wait again with the rest of us.

Another forty-five minutes later, our team of three was called forward.

Just us—and the clothes on our backs.

Everything else—our twenty-plus bags—had to wait with our hired Palestinian porters. Equipment. Jackets. Purses. Cameras. Fanny packs. Everything except what we wore.

We went through metal scanning machines and found ourselves let through to the other side—where we were enclosed in a cage surrounded by iron bars and wire fences. Beyond it, another set of heavy turnstiles—just out of reach.

We stood there, in the cage—having come through on their orders—and were ignored. For quite a long while.

Eventually, the Palestinian porters were instructed to pass all our cases of equipment over to us and return to their side of the border. They dutifully complied. (Can I just say—it was not easy to get the cases through the turnstiles.)

Then, we were three people in a cage with more than twenty cases of equipment.

After staring at us for what seemed like an eternity, one of the Israeli soldiers approached.

Well, he got as close to our cage as a fearful child might to a hungry lion at the zoo.

'Open your bags,' the young guard instructed, machine gun slung casually on his shoulder.

Which ones?

'All of them.'

'How can you inspect our bags from over there?' asked our reporter.

'We just can,' came the brusque reply.

What this apparently meant was that if they saw anything questionable from where they were, they'd have us take it out, walk as close to the bars as they'd let us, and hold up the suspect item.

'The fun hasn't even started,' the camerawoman whispered to me. She'd been here countless times before and wasn't surprised by this kind of greeting. 'We're not even at their x-ray machines yet.'

I had no idea where this was headed. But again, no space for fear.

After looking at all our gear from afar, we were asked for our passports and told to wait some more.

So—we waited.

And waited.

Meanwhile, the businesspeople and the mothers we had joined in the queue were also still waiting ... far behind us, on the Palestinian side.

For another hour or so, the Israeli soldiers just stared at us, looking tense and agitated. Humourless. Not that anyone could blame them. Just a few months before, the crossing was attacked by Hamas' first female suicide bomber, and she killed four Israelis as well as herself.

The very air around us sizzled with the mistrust between the sides. The silence was taut.

Then, from out of nowhere, that brittle quiet was broken. The Israelis started to sing. Seriously. They started to sing. First one guy, and then another. Until there was a full chorus of armed soldiers warbling songs in Hebrew. They were horribly off-key. It was torturous. Truly. A sound akin to cattle being slaughtered.

Our reporter was sitting on one of our twenty-some cases, and the shooter was on another. Neither was particularly thrilled at the surprise serenade.

'Do something,' the reporter said to me.

Excuse me? I thought.

'You're the producer—do something,' he repeated, half-jovial, half-hopeful.

I wasn't quite sure what to do. This seemed beyond my capabilities as a producer.

The Israeli singing only got louder. And more out of tune. As if they were doing it on purpose.

The reporter then made a strange request of me: 'Go on, sing.'

What? I asked, perplexed. *Are you nuts?!*

Firstly, he hated my singing. How did I know this? He told me. Numerous times. Or at least he pretended to hate it. I used to enjoy tormenting him on long car journeys by bursting into songs from *Fiddler on the Roof* since it was his least favourite musical. And in the journey through the desert to get to Gaza, I regaled him with a medley from *Jesus Christ Superstar*, which he seemed to equally abhor.

Not that he liked any musicals at all. (As you can see, we had a lot of time to talk and get to know each other on assignments.)

Then, here he was in Erez Pass *asking* me to sing. He must've snapped. There were guns pointed at us!

'Sing,' he said, again. 'It may lighten the mood—and drown out that awful racket they're making.' Ah, so there was method to his madness! And he wasn't just wanting to make me a target for the soldiers.

Pray tell, what do you want me to sing?—I asked, humouring him.

'Anything,' he replied. 'Anything at all. Maybe they'll warm to us and get us through quicker.'

Right. Sing. Ok, then.

'Think about it,' he invited, 'when else are you going to get a chance to sing at an Israeli border crossing—locked in a cage? You have the perfect captive audience here!'

Funny, I thought. Very funny.

'Imagine the stories we can tell afterwards—our Baghdad team manager will love this one—Gamra, singing at Erez Pass!' The twinkle in his eyes shone brighter than usual.

Fine. For this nutty reporter and our beloved news manager then.

I don't think I can be faulted for starting out with a squeak (Note: guns were pointed at us): 'Rivers belong where they can rammmmmmbbbbllleeee ...'

For some reason, trapped behind those iron bars, enclosed within those high blast walls with only a small window letting light in, 'Corner of the Sky' from *Pippin* felt—appropriate.

I then segued into a bit of 'Born Free' and 'Please Release Me (Let Me Go)'. (Yes, I was working around a theme.)

After a few tunes, our camerawoman joined in. With choreography.

We moved on to a new favourite duet: 'Build Me Up Buttercup'. We sang it together on the ride from Baghdad to Amman a week earlier. So, we were in practised, perfect two-voice harmony.

Our reporter—still seated on the edit pack case—was cracking up.

The Israeli guards began lowering their weapons and peering out of their high look-out posts to get a better view of what was happening in the cage beneath them.

It was apparent on their faces that they didn't know what to make of it.

I took this moment of confusion to give it all I had—and came out with my rendition of 'I Will Survive'. It was my anthem. I have sung that song in many odd locations. Including at the wake of a friend's father. (Believe it or not, it was at the family's request.) I had thought that the weirdest location of all—until a month prior to this Gaza trip, when I found myself singing it for the soldiers of the 1st A.D. at the Palestine Hotel lawn in Baghdad. (Long story!)

But then, Erez Pass. I think that trumps them all.

By the time I got to: 'go on now go, walk out the door ...,' the famous refrain of Gloria Gaynor's hit, the Palestinian porters behind the gate began singing along. The people trapped in the queue burst into cheer.

That's when the Israeli guards decide to fast-track us out of there.

What can I tell you? It's often said that **music is a universal language**. That dance tune definitely lightened the mood and made people smile.

That's what I recall most now about that tense and arduous crossing. I sang. People laughed. And suddenly, thanks to disco, we spoke one language.

Then, I ...

I was no longer petrified.

EUROPE

French Alps

Sometimes, you have to roll with it.

That Day in May

It was the end of the week and a slow morning at the office. That much I remember. But a search on the internet now tells me that an annular solar eclipse would be seen from Scotland the next day, and the Brits were beginning to investigate possible abuses by their soldiers in Iraq. Headline-making events. So, that 30th of May in 2003 *should've* felt like a busier day at the CNN London bureau—but the usual newsroom buzz was missing as many of the teams were already on their way to France for the G8 summit.

These summits are yearly 'informal' gatherings of leaders from the world's richest industrialized nations. They're usually forgettable and inconsequential—but the meeting in 2003 was anticipated to be slightly more interesting.

It was the year of George W. and Blair. Koizumi, Chirac, and Berlusconi. Gerhard Schroeder was the Chancellor of Germany.

Putin was already the Russian president, but no one had yet heard of Merkel. Or Macron, who was twenty-six then and still at university.

Looking back now, it seemed a simpler time. (Ah, the days of flip-top Nokia phones and a seemingly incontrovertibly united Europe.)

But the US led an invasion of Iraq a few months earlier. It greatly divided not just the G8, but public opinion across the globe. Admonitions and protests were expected—despite the summit's location being relatively remote to keep demonstrators away and the G8 leaders more secluded.

Not the Waters

The 2003 summit was in Évian-les-Bains, a ritzy spa town on the south shore of Lake Geneva in the Auvergne-Rhône-Alpes region in south-eastern France. The name alone evokes enchanting scenes of charming landscapes.

Évian is known for its (quite expensively bottled) mineral water and hypnotizing art deco and art nouveau buildings from the late nineteenth and early twentieth century. *La Belle Epoch,* and all that. The English Romantic poet Percy Bysshe Shelley and his wife Mary travelled through Évian in the early 1800s, before its transformation into a resort community. Mary Shelley, who wrote the renowned *Frankenstein,* set her famous character's first kill here.

In his own writing, Percy called Évian's inhabitants— wretched, diseased, and poor. Clearly, it was a very different town by the time the G8 summit was hosted.

At least, this is what I read.

As it Happened

That quiet Friday morning, two days before the summit, the newsdesk decided an additional back-up satellite truck was needed at the G8 to transmit video—or be on stand-by in case protests got bad. This was years before digital technology and the internet allowed for rapid-fire live feeds on handheld smart phones—so, a field team in a satellite truck had to physically drive through the winding roads of the French Alps to get as close as possible to Évian to transmit video back to the London broadcast centre. Why as 'close as possible'? Because it was past the deadline to get accreditation, and Évian was already secured, locked down, and chock-full of official G8 types and their coterie of assistants, industrialists, politicos, and, of course, *accredited* journalists. But this didn't deter the newsdesk editors at CNN. Nor did it put them off that there were few satellite trucks available because it was only two days before a major—*scheduled*—world event.

After several hours of mad scrambling, the desk eds found a truck in Eastern Europe. They hired a freelance crew to bring it across from Serbia to the G8. And they needed a CNN producer to join the freelancers and coordinate any network needs from the field. Guess who happened to be standing around the bureau doing not much else that early morning work shift?

Swiss Miss

So off I went to Switzerland, Geneva airport being closest to the summit location. I spent that first day wandering around the Swiss city alone, waiting for two Eastern Europeans to find me so we could drive across the border into France together.

Geneva was a very expensive place to wait in. An espresso cost nearly US$5. And this was in 2003! I didn't drink espressos, but it was the cheapest coffee I could get.

After wandering around the crisp, clinical city as much as I could, I sat by Lake Geneva nursing my expensive espresso for hours.

I sat and watched a high-powered jet shoot water straight up into the air, while Edwin and Isidora drove a satellite truck towards Geneva from Serbia. Heck, I wasn't complaining. I was looking forward to the Alpine adventure.

Springtime

Again, because we were lacking accreditation, the closest we could get to Évian was Morzine. A ski resort town two hours away. It was further inland and nowhere near Lake Geneva. I say two hours away because we were travelling in a satellite truck that could only go so fast. Especially with me having nowhere to sit.

You see: the little things—seemingly 'inconsequential' details—sometimes fall by the wayside. The CNN planner in London had presumed I could ride with the satellite crew. Without checking with them first.

The satellite crew wasn't told they had to 'transport' me until they were well on the road to Geneva.

The truck only had two seats.

Both were occupied.

If you've never seen a satellite truck from the early twenty-first century, let me describe it for you. It's big. Larger than a courier truck. In the front cab, there were built-in seats for the driver and one passenger. In back, there was a fully functional TV control room. Meaning there was a wide panel with an editing bay, a switcher with all sorts of buttons and levers, a wall covered in television screens and computer monitors, and in most cases, NO SEATS other than an office chair with wheels that allowed for quick movement across the back cabin, which was often necessary during live feeds. (Please note satellite trucks were always stationary when transmitting a signal.)

On long drives between gigs, the office chair was (sort of) held in place by a stretchy band 'tied' to the door.

This was the only other seat in the truck—and the one that I had to use.

A List

Problem #1: It was against the law to carry passengers in a vehicle unless they were in fixed seats.

Problem #2: We had to cross an international border and have our passports checked between Switzerland and France. The truck would come under inspection.

Problem #3: The stretchy band didn't really hold the chair steady at all, and we were zigzagging through the French Alps.

Do imagine how incredibly ridiculous I looked holding on for dear life to anything I could because the chair swivelled and rolled this way and that as the hulking satellite truck hurtled through the rugged mountain pass. It was like being on a roller coaster for two hours, non-stop. How my breakfast did not end up all over that control panel I will never know. The scene outside was stunning—at least from what I could tell.

It was June, in France. The sun was shining, the air was crisp. The Alps rippled a deep, lush green, and the striking cacophony of colours made everything take on the almost glossy sheen of an early twentieth-century technicolour film. A bit like the land of Oz in the 1930s Judy Garland movie. Blues never looked bluer, browns were deeper, and the sun literally gleamed gold. It's no wonder pioneer filmmakers Auguste and Louis Lumière had a holiday house here. Inspiration buzzed from every molecule of light in this stunning corner of Europe.

To be honest, I couldn't really appreciate the view as much as I hoped. There weren't many places to stop on the twisting mountain road without holding up traffic.

Edwin, who was driving, kept checking on me in the rear-view mirror. He gave up—early in the drive—trying to hide his laughter at the sight of me. He was laughing so much it made driving difficult. Apparently, I was later told, I looked like the ball in a pinball machine. Isidora, in the passenger seat, was cracking up, too.

For the remainder of the ride, all three of us were doubled-up in stitches at this ridiculous circumstance. Talk about unique bonding experiences.

Edwin and Isidora kept apologizing to me for the lack of better seating—when really, it wasn't anyone's fault. At least not anyone who was in the truck that day.

So, anyway …

We got to the border and the French guards inspected the truck. They walked around it, patted down panels and looked through every window. Then, a rather broad French guard pulled open the sliding door to the back cabin. I must admit I was slightly terrified.

Hardly breathing and rather dizzy, I sat there as still as possible, trying to keep from throwing up. My feet were acrobatically positioned to cover the rollers on the chair.

The guard looked at me. I looked at him, mouth firmly closed. My nausea was rising, and I hoped I didn't look like I was being smuggled across an international border.

A few tense awkward minutes of silence later, Edwin, Isidora, the satellite truck, and I were through into France on our way to Morzine.

And I can happily say that no one threw up that day.

Morzine

In June, without snow, hotel rooms were empty, most restaurants and services were closed, and everything seemed made of logs. Like a birthday cake that lacked icing to cover up the matchstick cabin decorations. In Morzine, those matchstick cabins are called chalets.

So, the satellite crew and I did a lot of waiting around in *chalets*. Which were just as cosy in the summer as they must be in winter.

We sat around and drank endless cups of much cheaper coffee, ate crepes to our hearts' content, and talked until the sun nearly rose again.

We also played pool in a place called 'Buddha Café'. It was billed as a cross between India and Pakistan, but it looked more like a Tibetan monastery's over-packed storage. Apparently, it was the hub of Morzine social life.

Every day, we waited to be called into action—and nothing.

Finally, on the last afternoon of the summit, we got a call to race to an airport where Air Force One, the US presidential plane, was waiting to depart. George W. was going to Egypt, and the CNN team travelling with him had a tape they needed played out to London while they were in flight. Yes, terribly unexciting stuff.

The Relay

I waited for the White House producer on the outside of the airport fence. He unceremoniously handed me a tape over the wire mesh as he rushed to keep pace with the departing American leader.

Tape in hand, I dashed back to the truck parked across the street to transmit the material to London for onward pass to CNN headquarters in Atlanta.

That was about as close to the action as I got on that assignment.

In half an hour, all that travel, all that waiting, all that pool, was over. Edwin and Isidora packed up the truck, dropped me off at another airport, and headed back to Serbia.

Moments

This was a long, roundabout way to tell you that sometimes (often), plans don't pan out. And sometimes (often), it's the waiting that matters. When life unfolds—despite your attention.

Had I let myself get anxious or panic or indeed question my 'purpose' on that assignment, I wouldn't have enjoyed a lovely three days travelling through the Alps with a charming pair of Eastern Europeans.

I never saw them again—Edwin and Isidora—but I will always remain grateful for the experience.

Sometimes (always), **going with the flow** is the journey's gift.

Poland

THERE'S MORE THAN ONE SHADE OF WHITE.

There is a softness to my memories of Poland. Tender light. And whispered colours. A gentle coolness to the images. Undemanding. And subdued.

It was 1995. I was a young reporter for a television newsmagazine show in the Philippines. We were invited by Poland's tourism ministry to visit their country and see how it had changed since the end of communist rule six years earlier.

It was my first time in Eastern Europe.

Blue, Grey, and White

Leafless trees were tall and crisp. The milky sky was sighing blue. Soviet blocks and Gothic corners slow-danced a tired triple-metre in muted mustard and the cobbled grey of broken hearts.

Winter tarried, but that's not the only reason Warsaw seemed colourless and dreary. Indelible traces of its painful past grasped every curve like the stale smell of mould in a room long unopened after its inhabitant has died. Murky water ran where snow melted, and prayers pooled in ancient gutters once drenched in blood.

Poland was trying to resuscitate itself after more than forty years behind the Iron Curtain. Before that, it spent five years under Hitler's brutal Nazi regime.

In 1995, Poland was not yet part of the European Union. But it wanted a place at that table and was angling to be recognized as progressive, cultured, and civilized.

Prism

Our news team of four from Manila were packed into a van with a Polish guide and driver. Together, we criss-crossed the country for several days.

Aside from wet and weary Warsaw, we were shown the simple beauty of Zakopane, a winter resort town at the base of the Tatra Mountains, near the border with Slovakia.

Zakopane was dotted with unique wooden chalets from the turn of the twentieth century, which showcased traditional construction and folk craftsmanship with art nouveau features. It was straight out of a travel guide. Even its churches were charmingly made of wood. The effect was stunning. More so as it was March and the entire town was draped in snow.

Further along, we stood transfixed before the miraculous image of the Black Madonna in Częstochowa. A venerated portrait of the infant Jesus and the Virgin Mary believed to be painted on wood from the table used at Christ's Last Supper.

Then, we were shown the sophisticated glories of Krakow. Reputably one of the most beautiful medieval cities in Europe.

Towards the end of our trip, we wandered in stunned silence at the horror of Auschwitz. The Nazi concentration camp was not on the original itinerary, but we asked to see it.

It's been decades since that visit and I still don't have the right words to describe the hallowed terror of that place. The haunted silence that echoed in the empty gas chambers. The brittle pain that reverberated in the rooms filled with hair shaved off hundreds of thousands of victims. The barbed wire barriers and fences that remained a testament to sharp hatred. Humanity at its worst. It's all there, enveloped in my memories of a sombre Polish winter.

I remember it almost in sepia, faded images of a faded time.

White Light

But in 1995, through that veil of grey, there was also a certain spark. For the first time in its history, the head of the Catholic Church, John Paul II, was Polish. Lech Walesa, iconic labour leader and Nobel Peace Prize winner, was president. Poland's people were hopeful about the future.

Fast forward. A decade later.

June.

Poland was on the eve of membership to the European Union. The country was still working through the nuances of its fledgling democracy—but was also beating the drum of globalization.

In Rome, the much beloved Polish Pope was dying.

In Krakow, where John Paul II was once archbishop, thousands of his countrymen came out to share their prayers.

Every evening, candles dressed the elegant city in a soft golden glow. The melting wax sticks lined the streets like miniature sentries standing guard over wilting flowers that had been plucked and gathered from every garden. An unkempt floral pavement.

Sadness whispered from every corner, and structured shadows played at archways and portals, enticing you to peek into its textured stories.

Outside the Archbishop's Palace, the faithful gathered, already in mourning. Many of them wore white. The colour of purity. The colour of the papacy. The colour of peace.

It was the colour of that Polish summer.

I was part of a CNN team sent to Krakow to wait for the inevitable.

White Noise

From my hotel room, you could see Wawel Castle. It stood on a slope, seemingly hunched from the weight of its history.

At night, it glistened like a bejewelled sovereign with its crown of dramatically lit gothic spires atop the gem-encrusted banks of the Vistula River.

Every morning, we wound our way around the disrobed castle to the church courtyard. It's where the faithful waited for news from Rome, so that's where the world's media, with our cameras and our platforms, waited too.

It's where 'the story' was.

By the end of the first day, there was no longer a line between the watchers and the watched. We, the watchers, occupied space and were in the way, so they (the watched) incorporated us into their reality. They laid candles and flowers on our platforms and fell to their knees in prayer around our tripods.

We, the media, became part of the snapshot of reality we were trying to capture for the daily news bulletins.

There was no resentment at our presence nor anger at the intrusion. As far as the faithful were concerned, we were white noise.

White Blanket

There was an overwhelming stillness that blanketed Krakow that early summer. The afternoons were dusted in the memory of soft kisses from a kinder sun, and a gentle nipping chill filled the air. It was as if the town itself had stopped.

People seemed to quietly set aside whatever social divisions there were and came together as members of a larger family. They gathered as one—in a silence cloaked in papal white.

A communal shield.

Something takes over when tragedy strikes. A sudden solidarity in shared fragility. A unifying sorrow when confronted with mortality.

There is something universal and binding about grief.

White March

Several days into the vigil for the ailing pope, the people of Krakow decided to walk in prayer through the streets wearing white.

As we filmed what was dubbed the 'White March', I was separated from our camera crew and found myself—unintentionally—in the middle of the procession.

Needless to say, I wasn't meant to be seen on camera as part of the march. I was there to witness, not participate.

But it was difficult to stay 'out of sight' when I had no idea where the camera was.

Regardless, I did my best under the circumstances to stay hidden while slowly making my way out of the crowd.

Have I mentioned that I was wearing a bright orange sweater?

Yup, in a sea of white, I was sort of hard to miss.

But the marching mourners didn't seem to mind my awkward bobbing and weaving as I walked among them.

Without a sound, we flowed together. Thousands of us silently cutting our own paths. Each putting one foot in front of the other, respectful of those around. Careful not to stand in each other's way.

We were all mindful of the company, and yet, each of us walked alone.

There was a certain peace to us all that summer afternoon.

There was a shared appreciation of being human.

White Movement

Some two decades on, and a very different Poland is in the news. And white has a whole other meaning.

Instead of hope or peace, it is blinding white heat. Spikes of anger and spears of division.

Right wing movements are on the rise and white supremacists are on the streets. Thrusting their skin tone ahead of themselves like a weapon.

We're back in the days of tribalism. Of 'us versus them'. Of 'ours is better than yours'.

It's 'an-eye-for-an-eye' or 'we-can-take-it-in-turn-so-long-as-I'm-first'.

Me first.

Me. Us. Them.

The swords of partition are drawn.

And it's not just in Poland.

White Space

I've learnt that at times like these—*because we have been here before*—it is more important than ever to listen to each other. To give people a blank page. A white sheet, a canvas.

To give each other *space*.

There is room for everyone who understands that there is space for all.

We seem to have forgotten that white only exists when there's an equal reflection of all visible light frequencies. Where one colour is no more prevalent or important than another.

Instead of using it as a token for hatred, it can be a symbol of compassion. Of humanity at its best.

I remember the horror of Auschwitz, and its shadows and barbed wire fences.

Then I hark back to the Polish pope dying in Rome.

The lines blurred that summer in 2005.

We walked in silence then in Krakow. Enfolded by a universal shield of humanity.

As I bobbed along in my bright orange sweater, I learnt **there is space for us all**—regardless of colour—in a communal sea of white.

Ireland

THERE'S ALWAYS TIME TO SEE THE CLIFFS.

It was the summer of 2004. I just got back to Europe after long, rotating assignments for CNN in the Middle East. There was a war on, and lives were ripped apart every day. So much violence and heartbreak is exhausting.

And it changes you.

I remember walking to work one morning and jumping behind a trash bin after a car backfired near me.

I was in Central London and thought I was being shot at.

It took me a while to get back up.

In Baghdad, where I had just come from, gunfire and explosions were a daily occurrence—and it wasn't just physically that they left their mark.

As you would've read earlier, on my last assignment there, two of our colleagues were killed in an ambush. One of them was a very dear friend.

I kept working stoically every day, then would wake up crying in the few hours I slept at night.

It was not an easy time.

Tidying Up

Shortly after the war in Iraq passed its one-year mark, US President George W. Bush—the man who ordered the initial assault—was travelling to Ireland for a summit with allies in the European Union. By then, eleven thousand people had been killed in the conflict, most of them Iraqi civilians.

At home, Bush was running for re-election, and this was to be his first official trip to Ireland, which then held the rotating presidency of the EU. The summit would not be taking place in the Irish capital, Dublin, but in the western county of Clare. It's where evidence of one of Ireland's earliest signs of human activity was found (dating back more than twelve thousand years), and it went on to be recognized for having the 'tidiest town' in the country.

Only staying the night, Bush was going to be put up in County Clare's prized location: Dromoland Castle. A medieval fortress turned exclusive golf resort thanks to the investment of Irish Americans.

The summit location meant that Bush would be landing at nearby Shannon Airport, which was controversially being used by US forces as a stopover and refuelling point to and from their battlefronts in Afghanistan and Iraq. The Irish public was none too pleased about that, feeling it made them complicit in wars they didn't support. And for the first time in modern history, a US president could not expect a warm Irish welcome. Especially as news had come out of US forces torturing and mistreating its prisoners in Iraq.

Two teams from CNN's DC bureau were travelling with the presidential party.

We were sent ahead from London to cover preparations and what went on around the official meeting.

More than 6,000 Irish forces were deployed to safeguard the location. It was the largest security operation they'd undertaken. Tanks rolled down roads leading to Shannon Airport and a wide cordon was established. Anti-war demonstrations had become customary around the US president. They followed him like the stench of poorly digested beans after a barbecue. There were rallies across the country and reports of thousands of protestors camping out just beyond the security line in County Clare. But Bush didn't see any of that.

We, however, were on stand-by for trouble.

Fortunately, there wasn't any. I'm not sure if it had to do with how well-guarded the summit was or the weather. It rained. Or as the Irish say: It was bucketing down.

From what we could see, people stayed home.

County Kerry

On the first day we were there, it was so quiet (news-wise) that we drove more than two hours from Clare to County Kerry to do a short report on the town. Simply because it had the same name as Bush's opponent in the upcoming presidential race.

None of us in the crew complained about the opportunity to do a little sightseeing. In our line of work, we didn't often get to see the best parts of a country.

In Kerry, we rode a horse-drawn carriage through the woods of Killarney Park and walked around crystal ebony lakes to see the ashen ruins of an ancient castle and a medieval abbey.

The sky was the colour of granite.

It was everything the reporter needed to put together a pretty little piece with a precarious political peg.

I don't recall much of what was said while we were filming, but what has stayed with me was the feel of the day. It was like we had stepped into a wonderfully bleary Irish postcard.

County Clare

The following morning—when the summit was actually happening—it was just as quiet. So quiet that our Irish driver offered to show us the sights closer to Shannon, within County Clare. So, in case we were needed for coverage, we wouldn't be too far away.

'Bad idea'—replied the cameraman. Insisting we stay put—'You never know.'

There was a three-hour window between our reporter's live shots. We were all just sitting in a rather empty conference room at an inn quite a distance from the official meeting. Our White House reporters were on-site, and there was not much for us to do on the fringes. There were no rallies, and no one was on the streets.

'Doesn't matter'—the shooter repeated—'I will wait right here.'

He waited alone. The rest of us took the driver up on his offer and left the inn. We didn't often get the opportunity for sightseeing when on assignment.

Moher

The trip through the Irish countryside was gorgeous. And it went by much faster than anticipated. In about half an hour, we approached the breath-taking Cliffs of Moher. Fourteen kilometres of rugged coastline dropping abruptly into the sapphire Atlantic Ocean. We were awe-struck by the majesty.

Bright green grass atop the naked splendour of shale and sandstone.

The cliffs looked like fossilized emerald waves.

There was no visitor centre, no cordoned off queues, and no ticket booths. We rucked right up to the edge of an overhang and gasped at the vastness of the tumultuous sea.

It was powerful. We were so high up that the horizon seemed to stretch into forever.

I never felt so small.

There was another producer with us who was just back from her first trip to Iraq. She was sent in after the ambush of our colleagues, joining a team still in mourning.

She was quiet for most of the drive to the cliffs.

She was quiet as we stood on the rise.

She was quiet. She was quiet.

She was quiet.

Then, suddenly, she was flat on the ground. Her face buried deep in the grass.

It took the rest of us by surprise.

I tried to help her up thinking she'd fallen. I was wrong.

She rolled over and turned her face to the sun. There were tears in her eyes … and a smile on her face.

None of us knew what to do.

Then, she turned again. And slowly, she crawled over to the edge of the cliff and peered out at the ocean.

'Grass,' she said, stroking the soft blades.

'And the sea,' she exclaimed, as if having just discovered water.

'Look at that,' she kept repeating. 'Look at that.'

Again, she rolled onto her back and smiled at the sky.

Then, she turned to me and laughed, tears streaming down her cheeks.

I looked into her eyes and understood.

We both spent time in an arid, empty, monochrome desert where hearts were crushed every day. Where pain burnt as harshly as the sun.

At the cliffs, a breeze whipped our hair and a welcome chill pinched our faces.

The day was soft, and the bright sky was a kinder, gentler blue.

'We're alive,' she said, as if sharing a new-found secret to happiness.

'We're alive,' she repeated, laying her head back on the ground.

I couldn't help but smile. She was right. We were alive. We survived another day. Many were not as fortunate.

Looking at her rolling around in the grass I was struck by how the world turns.

The world turns. And that is what matters.

It turns—and we humans keep going. Through conflict. Through inhumanity. Through heartbreak.

But standing on those Irish cliffs I was reminded that we must also take the time to stop—and appreciate life's majesty.

The tumult of the ocean, the ruggedness of the ground.

The colour of the sky.

We are alive, and **there is always time to see the sights. To find the joy and be grateful.**

'Time to go!' the driver's cry broke into our reverie.

I helped my colleague up then and hugged her as she wiped away her tears.

'We're alive,' she whispered again in my ear.

There is not much else I need to recall about that trip.

SOUTHEAST ASIA

The Mainland

IF YOU FOLLOW THE RIVER, YOU'LL MAKE IT HOME.

You know how explorers through the ages have been able to navigate by knowing their position in relation to the North Star? That's how I feel about rivers. Everywhere I go, I gauge where I am by proximity to the river. All the world's greatest cities have one coursing through them. And throughout history, human civilization has flourished along waterways.

I am not sure what it is about rivers that attracts me. Maybe it's knowing that I am in a metropolis but not landlocked? No matter how narrow the channel, a river offers some breathing room—you can step back and take in a view of where you're at—while at the same time reminding you that there is more than what you see. After all, rivers do lead to the sea. They're like signposts showing you the exit—or pointing you to a great beyond.

When I lived in London, it was always by the Thames. I'd walk its banks to the office or sit by its rushing waters with a cup of coffee and write. Even in the winter. And on days I wasn't particularly at my best, I'd follow the river and inevitably feel better by the time I reached Tower Bridge on its east end. Simply because I had taken the time to breathe.

This was a rather fluvial way to tell you about Phnom Penh and peninsular Southeast Asia, what I enjoyed best about being there, and what it taught me.

Where Rivers Meet

Phnom Penh, the Cambodian capital, sits at the junction of the great Mekong and Tonle Sap rivers, which converge before emptying into the South China Sea.

When there on assignment, I looked forward to meals along the riverbank or grabbing a coffee—just as I did in London—and taking in the city.

The legendary Mekong is the longest river in Southeast Asia—twelfth longest in the world—running 4,000 kilometres from China through five countries on its way to the sea. While the Tonle Sap is the only river on the planet of which the tide reverses every year.

At the end of the rainy season, when the waterflow from the Mekong is strongest, the Tonle Sap is directed away from the sea to run instead into what is Southeast Asia's largest freshwater lake. Also called Tonle Sap. One of the most vibrant ecosystems in the world.

It's from here that the ancient Khmer Empire prospered, ruling over continental Southeast Asia from 800 CE for six centuries. Renowned for their construction skills, the Khmer built vast temples reflecting both Buddhist and Hindu influences. The most famous being Angkor Wat, the largest religious monument in the world, which sits on a site that's nearly 200 acres. One afternoon, after filming, we got the chance to rush through the temple complex before it closed. Nowhere near enough time, but you take what you can get.

Angkor Wat is stunning. (And yes, I realize I am using that word a lot in this book. But there is much in this world that is beautiful. Man-made and otherwise.)

I digress.

Back to the Mekong and the Khmer. So, Continental Southeast Asia—where they ruled—is now five countries: Cambodia, Thailand, Vietnam, Laos, and Myanmar. Distinct cultures that share land or fluvial borders. The tail end of the peninsula forms part of Malaysia, the rest of which is maritime territory.

The Southeast Asian maritime states—the Philippine islands, Indonesia, Singapore, East Timor, Brunei, and Malaysia—have a very different experience to the mainland nations. Surrounded by water, their land territories are rather more clearly defined.

On *peninsular* Southeast Asia, though the countries are demarcated, the lines have changed through the centuries, and the people are like the Mekong. Fluid and unmindful of borders.

Cambodia | Vietnam

We met the Leung family on their houseboat in Phnom Penh. They were preparing to celebrate Vietnamese New Year, just like hundreds of other Vietnamese residents on Cambodia's Tonle Sap. Besides being an occasion to honour their ancestors, the three-day celebration marks the start of spring. There's lots of feasting, drinking, and socializing. And those who celebrate make it a point to stay welcoming and optimistic during the festival, believing it sets the stage for good fortune the rest of the year.

But while preparing the traditional meal, Leung Ti Neung told us she didn't *feel* Vietnamese.

Like hers, many families from across the international border had lived in Cambodia for generations. Legally or otherwise. They'd come down the Mekong from Vietnam in pursuit of opportunities.

At the time we met the Leungs, the government estimated there were over a million Vietnamese people living within Cambodian borders. And despite the family's optimism, it was not an easy co-existence.

Many of Ti Neung's ethnic Khmer neighbours still saw her people as outsiders. Referring to such migrants as 'savages'.

There's a long, complex history between the two peoples—as is typical of fluvial neighbours.

But here's the thing: as much as there were underlying tensions and discrimination against Vietnamese migrants, we also met Cambodians who regularly crossed the border to Vietnam for healthcare. Illegally. There was a lack of domestic health centres to cater to their needs, and the few private hospitals that existed were too pricey. They relied on the 'savages' for help then and were deeply grateful. When people are in need, there is no holding them back from getting it met.

For the Leungs, the relationship between their people and the Khmers all had to do with mindset—which was fluvial. It had gone through so many ups and downs that it was like the Tonle Sap. And in keeping with Vietnamese New Year tradition, the family remained optimistic that given time, it would again change direction.

Cambodia | Thailand

Some three hundred kilometres north of Phnom Penh, a lesser-known river literally served as part of the border between Cambodia and another neighbour, Thailand. It wound through crop fields and forests. People on either side were oblivious to the national boundaries, until a gun battle broke out between their armies over a nearby ancient monument.

Preah Vihear, a Khmer temple dating back to 500 CE, had been ruled over the centuries by each country. At one point or another. In 2008, it was listed as a UNESCO World Heritage Site, deemed for universal conservation due to its significance in human history. Though thrilled at the development, Thailand and Cambodia were still at odds over land around the temple, as whoever got control would also benefit from the boost in tourism.

The temple itself was recognized in the 1960s by the International Court of Justice as part of Cambodia, much to the dismay of Thailand.

The Thais had built a paved road that led to the ruins, but that entrance was shut and the trek from the Cambodian side—which had access—was so much more difficult. Involving the need for a 4x4 vehicle, muscle strength, and patience.

After a three-hour-or-so drive past rice fields, through rubber and tobacco plantations, and former territory of the dreaded Khmer Rouge, we turned into a rough dirt road that seemed to stretch on for hours more. Jostled and tossed inside the vehicle, I was too busy holding on to whatever I could to keep proper track of time.

There were several checkpoints up the mountain range to Preah Vihear. Then, we had to walk the last stretch of narrow road to the temple complex, alongside monks garbed in orange robes and heavily armed soldiers. It was an odd mix. But one, we were told, that people there were used to.

At the entrance to the site, there were rows of barbed wire that had been hastily put up to fence the two peoples apart.

The locals told us there used to be a market just on the other side of the temple, busy with vendors and buyers from both sides of the border. Each freely exploring the other's wares—but not anymore.

For them, the concerns of national arguments were far away … all that mattered was the temple and their day to day.

The temple itself was spectacular, with numerous gateways and columns still standing. Carved out of the mountain, the stonework featured ornate trimmings and Hindu deities. The blue and red flag of modern Cambodia looked so small waving in the wind amongst the ancient grandeur.

As the cameraman filmed, I wandered around taking everything in—until I noticed that I seemed to have got in his way. Hurrying to get out of shot, I took a wee tumble down a rather steep flight of stairs.

I was carrying the boom mic and a notebook, neither of which I wanted to drop (priorities), so I broke my fall with my knuckles and landed on my knees. Took me a while to realize I was bleeding—even through my trousers.

I still have the scars from stumbling down those ancient stairs. But boy was the view from where I landed amazing. Expansive and verdant. Overlooking Cambodian fields and Thai plateaux. Which sparkled under the golden light of the tropical sun like one—seamless—blessed landscape.

View From the Other Side

We were on this story from both sides of the border, and it was on the Thai side that we encountered some trouble. There was a protest and it got violent. But it was Thais turning on Thais.

People from the cities had descended on the small border town wanting to impose their offended sense of nationalism over the temple. But those who lived on the border were not moved by the 'patriotic' intrusion.

Nor were the farmers and cricket hunters we met further down by the boundary river. In places, the river was so narrow they could have one foot in Cambodia and the other in Thailand—and they just wanted to keep earning a living without fear of bullets whizzing by.

For them, lines on a map could not enforce a sense of separation. Nor could markers be used to create a communal bond.

(Side note: It was here that I was bitten by a dengue mosquito. Made little difference on which side of the river it happened. I ended up spending two weeks in a hospital, in a whole other country! Not fun.)

Thailand | Myanmar

North of its Preah Vihear border with Cambodia, Thailand shares a boundary with Myanmar. A stretch of which is defined by the Moei River. Another waterway I remember well. We spent quite a bit of time along its banks in the Thai city of Mae Sot. Waves of people were coming across every day fleeing oppression and poverty in Myanmar. When the water was low, they could even make the trek on foot. They were not turned away. The Thais worked with their local government to offer refuge.

A Long Way from the Tigris

Late one evening, I was finishing a script in my Mae Sot hotel room when there was a pounding on my door like thunder. My heart leapt to my throat, and I froze. Then, a very familiar voice I hadn't heard in years called out my name. To my surprise, it was a dear friend from Baghdad! An old colleague from CNN. He got to chatting with a guy in the lobby who turned out to be my cameraman. He bolted for my room as soon as he was told I was the network's correspondent on the story.

A small Thai border town was the last place either of us had imagined for a reunion. Talk about a long way from the Tigris to the Moei!

To go even further back, he was raised in Ostrava where the Ostravice River flows—and I in Manila by the Pasig.

Just a reminder that people's *stories* are not cut and dried, and eventually, we all flow into each other.

Indonesia

One of my early reports for Al Jazeera was on the world's most polluted river—the Citarum in Western Java. It was a dead waterway, stagnant and brown, which had once been the birthplace of another ancient kingdom.

Along its historic banks, we met a skinny man with a floppy hat named Pepen, who was scavenging through rubbish with his young son. Pepen recalled that the Citarum had once been full of fish—but that was no longer the river his son was growing up with.

Instead, the waterway was choked with industrial waste, domestic refuse and sewage, and—as Pepen told us—dead bodies.

The river also fed the largest power generator in Java, Indonesia's most populous island.

Basically, the Citarum supported the food, water, and electricity supply for some twenty-five million people.

The national government promised to clean it up—but over a decade later, Citarum retained the title of world's worst river. And it's a problem for just one country. All 200 miles of it only course through Indonesia. Those who live along its banks share a national identity. A very different experience to fluvial residents in mainland Southeast Asia.

Dinnertime

One night, I was having dinner with a multinational crew along the river in Bangkok. Present were our local producer, the Indonesian shooter I worked with in Citarum, and another colleague from Singapore. We spoke about identity and how each one saw the others—the entire conversation was in English.

Seemed none of us fit the others' cultural expectations. Which led to questions about how and why people even need to pin these things down.

I can't tell you the number of times I have been asked where I am from, and when the reply doesn't conform to the expectation, there are always follow-up questions. But you see, if you keep unravelling it, there are endless answers to where one comes from. And ultimately, we are all likely to lead back to the same source.

On that assignment, our multi-fluvial team had a common goal. And we worked together to accomplish it regardless of our origins.

From the Pasig to the Thames, the Tigris, the Mekong, the Tonle Sap ... there are reminders everywhere of life's fluidity and confluence. The world is so large, yet small at the same time ... everything is connected and in constant motion, and nothing—not even identity—is set in stone. Not national borders, communal memories ... nor animosity.

The key is **to stay open and trust the flow**, then it's easier to **be at ease with who you are** ... and where you go.

NORTH ASIA

South Korea

WHEN YOU CLEAN UP THE OIL, YOU MAY FIND THE PEARL.

Bubble gum and popsicle hues. You know the ones I mean. Bright, fresh, exuberant. Soft lemon yellows, plush pastel pinks, bouncy baby blues. The kind of tones that work best when you're a teen. Even the black, white, and greys have a polish. A layer of sophistication that doesn't dull the enthusiasm.

That's what now springs to mind when I think of South Korea. The poppiest of Pop Culture. The trendiest of trends. Novelty at its peak. The South Koreans have managed to export a carefully curated edition of their identity, with which the world has fallen in love. It's soft power at its strongest.

There's K-pop music, K-dramas, K-lifestyle, even K-food and K-alcohol. It's an entire K-ultural movement.

From the global record-breaking singing groups BTS and Blackpink to TV fan favourites *C.L.O.Y.* and *Goblin*, and the multi-awarded international sensations *Parasite* and *Squid Game*. In less than a decade—like an infestation of shiny rainbow-coloured moss—the South Koreans have very intentionally K-aptivated the world.

Beyond Kimchi

In 2006, when Al Jazeera English first went to air, outsiders seemed to know little about the country that wasn't related to the dictator to its north, religious fanatic Moonies, or Samsung, which had just become the world's top producer of televisions. A few people might have already heard about kimchi and the country's rapid economic growth—referred to as a 'miracle'—but there were still those who thought South Korea formed part of China or Japan. Shocked that it had a vibrant culture of its own.

At the time, Al Jazeera didn't have a bureau in Seoul, so our team was over quite regularly from Manila.

On our first assignment, the South Korean capital was just getting a shot of adrenalin. 'Rejuvenation' was all the talk around town, and there was a multitude of rehabilitation projects. Derelict areas were being made over and quiet parts of town were receiving a boost. It was a city coming out of hiding, re-touching its make-up.

To me though, Seoul already appeared crisp, clean, and composed. Cosmopolitan yes, but also, in a way, a tad clinical. It exuded efficiency but seemed cold. Slightly aloof. Holding visitors at arms' length. The country itself was still a way from embracing the cool, inviting energy it would soon emit to the world. Not that I was complaining. Our trips over were always interesting. And there was so much to learn about what lay beneath the surface.

Sub-Seoul

For some reason, Seoul reminded me of Madrid. Maybe it was the areas with boxy brick buildings and the tree-lined streets. Or the elegantly dressed urbanites. I can't explain it.

The two places are nothing alike really, considering their historical and cultural influences couldn't be more different. Not to mention their geography. Expanding out from the banks of the Han River, Seoul has gentle slopes and is hilly in parts, while Madrid is generally flat and the only capital in the world without a waterway.

But then again, those are externalities.

I Now Pronounce You ...

The call for us to pack our bags came from the newsdesk in Doha when the cameraman and I were off duty and at a morning wedding in Manila. A crane barge had collided with a crude carrier off the coast of Taean County, about two hours south of Seoul. It led to the worst environmental disaster in South Korea's history. Nearly 11,000 tonnes—2.8 million gallons—of oil leaked into the Yellow Sea. Affecting one of Asia's largest wetlands, damaging hundreds of sea farms, and spoiling some of the country's most visited beaches.

The oil spill devastated communities dependent on tourism and selling seafood.

The cameraman with me at the time was on secondment from our Indonesian bureau—and all he had with him were clothes suitable for the tropics.

It was winter in South Korea and temperatures were below freezing. Neither of us was prepared.

Pressed for time, we were told to just pick up anything we needed once in country. We had to be on the first flight out of Manila, which was later that same afternoon.

It was December 2007.

As soon as we landed in Seoul, we were picked up in a van by a local crew and driven to Taean County. We only stopped for essentials when we were close enough to the site of the oil spill to not worry about traffic slowing us down.

The only establishment open was a very small fishing store, with a rather limited choice of products.

My colleague and I ended up with matching wellies and coats, dressed like twins for the entire assignment.

Apparently, we looked like variations of Gumby—think the dull-green clay figure in small and XXL.

Nope, I am not old enough to remember the original 1950s animation—the resemblance was pointed out to me by a desk editor who was feeling humorous.

Clay and Oil

But there was nothing funny about what we encountered in Taean. Over twenty kilometres of coastline ruined by oil as deep as ten centimetres.

Tar balls were washing ashore then dropping to pollute the seabed.

All sorts of wildlife were killed from being covered in oil.

There was just so much of it. The crude. We were overwhelmed by its sulphuric smell even before reaching the coast. The van taking us had all its windows up and yet the stench of petrol crawled into our nostrils like molasses. It was nauseating.

When we got closer, we saw the surface of the sea solid black, unceasingly inching towards the shore like rubber.

It was not easy to work while breathing that in.

But work the volunteers did. More than a million people came from across the country to help gather the spill and clean the beaches. They combed through sand and carefully wiped down surviving birds and individual rocks.

Using anything they could, volunteers filled containers with oil for removal. It seemed a futile endeavour. Like the Dutch Boy in the old children's story, using a finger to plug a hole in a dam and stop it from bursting.

Except here, the 'dam' had already burst, and the 'boy' was desperately trying to push the leak back in.

Their determination was commendable. Within a month, they'd managed to collect a third of the total oil spilled.

Live From …

We reported from Taean's Mallipo Beach, a popular resort town turned ghost town in the dead of winter. Everything was shuttered. And the oil spill just made it bleaker.

There was no place to stay, but the local producer found us what may or may not have been a small hostel—or it was someone's house. I am still not sure. Basically, it was somewhere to at least lay our heads at night. Even if there was no escaping the smell of sulphur.

During the day, we worked out of a small store that usually sold oysters. The mollusc was among the town's most valuable products. But at that point, Mallipo's oysters were coated in petrol.

Overall, the clean-up was estimated to have cost more than US$300 million, involving more than 300 vessels—sea and aircraft—and around 20,000 military personnel, aside from the civilian volunteers.

Eventually, tugboat captains were imprisoned for criminal negligence, but that did little for the town's recovery.

For years after the spill, tourism was all but dead. The ecosystem was damaged, and sea farmers and fisher folk struggled to revive their businesses.

On a Winter's Day a Traveller

One morning, we drove away from the oil-drenched coast and up a hill to get a broader view of the affected community. We wanted to see how people were doing away from the clean-up efforts, and to visually capture the juxtaposition of snow-white slopes and slick black sea.

We couldn't spot a soul. It was so intensely quiet.

Then, we got to a bend where the snow was freshly disturbed. A person seemed to be walking away. Leaving a new tombstone standing against the silence.

It turned out to be the end of a burial. A family man—an oyster farmer—had killed himself. His daughter said he saw no way out from under the oil and wanted to spare his loved ones the failure. His family was bereft. Angered too by his decision. It was heartbreaking.

I learnt then that South Korea has for years had one of the highest suicide rates in the world. Despite its prosperity and appearances of social integration, many people were feeling disconnected, left out of the growth miracle and national success. The despondent father was one of them.

Such a rapid economic rise could not possibly have come without tons of pressure. And the South Koreans were feeling it despite the glossy image.

According to South Korean psychologists, the seemingly 'better' things got, the more pressured people felt to 'perform'. To keep their best foot forward. Especially as it's a society where identity remains largely dependent on community perception.

Suicide rates also rose among Korean celebrities. Stoking concerns about copycat actions. As a local paper put it: If the stars couldn't hack it, what hope was there for mere mortals?

All in the Gutter

Social pressure and mental disquiet are of course not unique to South Korea. It's a global ailment. The more advanced our societies—and the more interconnected—the more stress and anxiety we seem to have created for ourselves.

Take, for example, the development of power and electricity. It brought on industrialization and modernity, but also led to the depletion of the earth's resources.

Similarly, it seems the more widely information has become available, the less people have wanted to learn. It's almost like the access to knowledge has instead prompted many to choose to stay within the safety and confines of ignorance.

Undeniably, globalization is a human triumph—but it's come with obvious challenges. Among them, it's exacerbated the urge to compare and compete.

We see it across something as ostensibly benign as social media. What was meant to keep people in touch and in tune with each other has led to increased angst, self-doubt, and insecurity. The need to 'belong' in the most superficial of ways has gone viral. There's an impassioned drive to be 'as good as' because we see ourselves as 'not enough'.

But we are enough.

You are enough.

As am I.

Even if we don't make public any private struggles or individual accomplishments.

We must take better care of our personal spaces and not let the virtual world dictate how we feel about our lives. (Note to self!)

And it would be good to check in with each other in the *real* world and make sure people know they're not alone.

Psy-ed Story

In 2012, a performer called Psy—arguably the first Korean superstar—took over popular imagination. He was everywhere!

A satirical entertainer, Psy was middle aged, portly, and unlike any of the carefully moulded, highly stylised K-pop stars that followed, but he will always be the world's first taste of K-pop culture.

And he didn't come from out of nowhere. Psy was a long-standing comic known domestically for poking fun at social mores.

Particularly in 'Gangnam Style', he derides the extent people go to affect pretences—while himself coming from the affluent community of their aspirations.

The catchy (awful) tune, with matching dance moves, was #1 globally and hailed a cultural phenomenon. The Secretary General of the UN went as far as calling it a 'force for peace'.

At the height of Psy's international fame, relations between the two Koreas were at a low point. The north had yet again upped its threat of a nuclear attack. As part of our coverage of the tension, we had to attend a Psy concert. Truly.

Psy would be releasing his next album at the show, and in a global first, the whole performance would be streamed live online.

Security was so high at the open-air stadium that there were military choppers overhead.

Despite fears, the venue was packed. And the show—I must say—was amazing. All flash and glitz.

There were aerial feats and jaw-dropping performances like I'd never seen. But there was more going on that evening than an historic musical event—and everyone in the crowd knew it. Psy himself said he planned to be loud enough to be heard in North Korea.

It was defiance in the face of intimidation—and a confidence in the courage of life.

End Note

I may see South Korea now in the manner it has carefully K-rafted, but I have not forgotten another lesson it taught me—that there are things appearances don't convey. Like the Psy concert, with its blinding lights, security choppers, and sleight of hand, there's more than can be seen with the naked eye.

Years later, the mayor who rejuvenated Seoul became the nation's president, then was disgraced and imprisoned for corruption. The chart-topping performer/clown stepped back from the spotlight an alcoholic—and I've kept my promise to myself to always **take the time to look beneath the surface.**

I will never forget that biting morning on a snow-covered mountain, with a beach that was black with oil. A family grieved the loss of their father before the New Year, because he lost all hope underneath an oyster farm drenched in crude.

Japan

There's nothing like the strength of paper walls.

There are assignments that become part of your DNA. If you've read this far, you'll know that for me, being in Iraq and Gaza are among them. This was another one.

3/11

As I write this, it's been more than a decade since the 11th of March 2011, also referred to as 3/11. A date etched not only in Japan's collective memory, but in those who watched the inescapable torrent of shocking videos that captured it. Cars like pebbles swept away by churning apocalyptic waters, homes like uprooted flowers on broken earth, and countless lives destroyed beyond recognition.

Japan was struck by a triple whammy like no other country has been subjected to. A tremendous **earthquake**, which triggered a massive **tsunami** that then damaged a **nuclear power plant**. All rolled up into one traumatic ball.

The quake was so strong it moved parts of the country 2.4 metres closer to North America. More than 19,000 people were killed and entire communities were wiped out, leaving nearly half a million people displaced.

The resulting tsunami reached a height of forty metres and travelled up to ten kilometres inland at a speed of over seven hundred kilometres per hour. It even shifted waters in Norway! It's no wonder a purportedly safe nuclear plant was damaged.

The images are burnt in my mind. And soon after seeing it on TV, our team was on the ground in Sendai. Nearby airports were damaged, so we drove over from Tokyo.

The devastation was indescribable. The world had been turned upside down, and everywhere lay reminders that nothing was as understood. Mangled cars sat atop dislocated roofs. Tons of fish were scattered on streets like buntings after a parade, and boats were perched precariously among shattered shop fronts. There were endless mountains of debris so mutilated they looked like piles of matchsticks left to mark where towns once stood.

That's but a short list of what was at least tangible. The intangible damage was immeasurable.

The sea that nourished them had become a traitor, and the nuclear energy that for decades was a blessing had become a curse.

It was like being trapped in a 4-D horror movie with no ending. Not even a pause button.

And yet, no length of film could capture the immensity of Japan's triple tragedy.

New Landscape

Along the country's north-eastern coastline, as far as the eye could see, a new landscape emerged so incomprehensible that survivors wandered around wordlessly for days trying to take it all in. It had become hallowed ground, and they anxiously searched among the wreckage for missing relatives.

The sacred silence was such that their footfalls echoed like canons at a state funeral.

Despite the overwhelming loss, people's hope for the future was never extinguished. This was Japan's worst ordeal since World War II, but there was no question of *if* it would recover— only *when*.

Kamikaze

Let me jump three months later to June. The harsh winter was making way for spring.

We met 'Sato' in a small hotel room in Fukushima with traditional tatami grass mat floors. He sought refuge behind seemingly fragile shoji panels and the darkness loaned by drawn curtains.

It was a warm, sunny afternoon. And we huddled together as if in a confessional.

He didn't want to divulge his full name, and I only remember his face in shadow. But that mattered little. What he would tell us—within those paper walls—encapsulated the spirit of a nation.

Sato was one of the hundreds working in shifts around the clock to try and contain the numerous leaks at the crippled nuclear power plant. A 'human wave', he called it.

They'd been at it since the 11th of March, risking their lives exposed to high levels of radioactivity, and going for months without even knowing if their own families had survived.

Sato spoke through a translator and only said one line in English: 'We are kamikaze.' They knew they were on a suicide mission. And his voice was tinged with both sadness and dignity.

Sato had worked at the nuclear plant for over ten years, and said its problems stemmed from design flaws. Its original American makers built it to withstand tornadoes and hurricanes— which are prevalent in the US. But the design hadn't been adapted for tsunamis nor earthquakes, which are what Japan is prone to.

Sato didn't want to waste time pointing fingers. What he seemed most intent to do was take accountability for allowing people to 'blindly believe' in what he called the 'myth of infallible safety'.

He felt responsible for letting people think that the nuclear plant was safe. And so, he was sacrificing his life to atone for what he saw as his wrongdoing.

In Fukushima, many were displaced not because of the quake but the danger posed by a leaking nuclear plant.

It may have been extreme in Sato's case, but it was common for people to be conscious of their responsibility to their community.

One for All

We met a mother in an evacuation centre who told us that after they'd gotten a safe distance away, she made her two young sons watch as the tsunami devoured their village below. That way—she explained—when it happens again, they would already understand the power of nature. So, they would not be rattled by it and be better able to help their neighbours.

Both sons had been having trouble sleeping ever since, but their mother believed the trauma would ultimately make them stronger.

The children's father had been working at sea when calamity struck, and they hadn't seen him since. Weeks later, he walked into their evacuation centre. The waves had carried him far, and in his subsequent search for his family, he'd stumbled upon strangers in need of help. So, he cared for them first. Trusting that had his family survived and needed assistance, no one would hesitate to provide it.

This strong sense of community permeated most of the 3/11 survival stories we heard.

Respect

In the school gymnasiums and courtyards that served as temporary shelters for those displaced, thousands of families used what they could to make small enclosures for themselves. Mindful of respecting each other's privacy. Shoes were neatly lined up by the entrance, and disinfecting liquids were readily available. Everyone wore surgical masks, careful not to pass anything on to those most vulnerable among them. Food distribution was organized, and the residents themselves devised cleaning rotas. They worked together like a well-oiled machine, without any of the chaos we'd seen in other locations of communal tragedy.

And we saw no one—not a single person—put themselves ahead of their neighbours.

Onward

'Mine is not the only pain here.' Another unforgettable survivor told us. Tomoyuki Murakami. A civil servant who was trapped atop city hall in Rikuzentakata after the calamity. He later found out that he'd lost his mother and his young son. But he carried on working, overseeing the erection of temporary shelters. Aware that his community—among the most devastated in Japan—was relying on him.

'I have to keep working to move us forward,' he said.

That's what they all seemed determined to do. There was little other choice. Life goes on, they kept repeating, and they refused to drown in the immensity of their bereavement.

So, they worked to rebuild. And shared the load.

Hundreds of others came from unaffected areas to volunteer their time and their services, seeing it as a matter of human duty.

Construction workers, counsellors, engineers, and even lawyers like Yukimitsu Saitu.

'So many have lost the foundation of their lives,' Saitu said. 'People are damaged in all kinds of ways, and I am here because it is important to support each person's problems, one-on-one.'

Saitu spent his free time going to evacuation centres helping survivors deal with the legal issues so often overlooked in such calamities. Mortgages. Debts. Inheritance. Insurance. Death certificates. To offer concrete solutions to concrete concerns.

And no one was expected to have all the answers. Even the fledgling national government—newly installed at the time—was given leeway regarding any shortcomings, on the understanding that what had happened was beyond simple human comprehension.

Through it all, there were constant aftershocks. Over a thousand. The worst ranged from 7.1–7.4. And we were there for a big one.

It struck close to midnight. We had just finished dinner and were preparing to turn in when the ground began to lurch. It was like being trapped in the bowels of a ship in tumultuous seas during a tornado. The concrete walls shook like tatami, and objects were falling off tables. It was nearly impossible to stay upright. Again, I felt like a pinball in an arcade game, jostled from side to side, expecting to drop through a surprise abyss.

After the Shock

Despite what's said, life didn't flash before my eyes at such a confrontation with mortality. There was no rifling through memories of the past or worrying about the unknowable future. The senses were heightened, anchoring you in the inescapable present. And everything seemed to happen in slow motion. At any second, the ground could give way beneath you, the world could crash down from above—and there was nothing you could do about it.

Nothing.

I can't even imagine what that was like for those who survived the 9.1 megaquake just weeks earlier. They were already on unsteady ground.

The jolt of that aftershock, an unnecessary reminder dared we think that life was in our control.

House of Cards

For me, Japan brought home the message that we reside in a house of cards. With perishable tatami floors, translucent shoji paper panels, and tree bark roofs. Purposeful, but fragile. Providing the illusion of privacy in an interconnected world.

It's easy to forget and think we're on solid ground, but really, nothing is unbreakable. Everything is in motion, in constant flux—even if we don't see it or feel it. The universe is relentlessly evolving—that's what it means to be alive.

How funny, we humans. Our greatest gift—the interminable instability, the impermanence, the constant opportunity for change—and all we do is try to pin things down. Finally accepting defeat on that matter could be our greatest triumph.

A Bento Blessing

In Japan, I saw the effectivity of dealing only with what's in front of you, trusting that all else will work out as best it can.

The quake survivors didn't indulge in moments of powerlessness—which they might have felt had they worried about things that were out of their hands.

We were staying in a town left standing near the disaster zone. It offered a place to sleep and have our meals. But the aftershock took away power, and no stores or restaurants were open.

Within hours, a boxful of food was brought to where we were doing live shots on the street—from a resident who'd taken it upon himself to feed those without. We thanked him for his generosity and offered to pay, suggesting he give the food to those who'd lost their homes. He reassured us that he had meals for them as well. This box—he repeated—was prepared for us. He considered us neighbours, since we were there too, telling the world their story.

Fast Forward

How does one move past the multiple catastrophes of 3/11? I spoke to a Japanese woman at the time who put it thus: It isn't so much what you **do** (to survive)—it all depends on **who** you **are**.

The devastated region rebuilt its communities in less time than expected. And a decade later, the debris swept out to sea from Japan was still washing up on shores across the Pacific.

No borders or oceans can truly separate what's connected— and any dividers we raise will always only have the strength of paper walls.

Mongolia

WHEN IT'S COLD OUT, THE GOAT
STAYS INSIDE THE GER.

I remember Mongolia in royal hues. A seamless stretch of bright deep blue raised over an infinite ermine landscape. Such a bold cold wilderness had never looked more stunning.

The air was crisp, almost brittle in its sharpness, and outside of the capital Ulaanbaatar—it was also clean.

I'd never seen so much ... space. Just *blank* space.

From the moment we landed, we were enveloped by emptiness.

My mother had just died, and the scenery seemed to reflect my emotional state.

It was the dead of winter, the coldest time of the year in a country of extreme temperatures.

We arrived to a very grey day. And the chill was a heavy haze suspended over the terrain. I brought an old iPod with me for comfort on the journey, and I filled the silence with Demi Lovato on loop singing 'Let it Go' from the movie *Frozen*. (Could I have been more on the nose?) For two weeks straight that was all I listened to, even when the sky was back to a blinding blue. There's just something about pop music—overly cheesy or not—that buoys me. Maybe it's the underlying simplicity of it or its youthful exuberance—it is what it is without pretension. Pop songs were always a sort of *balm*, if you will, from the gravity of news.

And if not pop, I listened to showtunes.

But Mongolia—with its extensive starkness and numbing embrace—was dedicated to Demi Lovato's 'Let It Go.' It got me through filming eight distinct stories in eight days while grieving. That's a lot. We were only slated to produce six reports in the two weeks we were there, but when additional opportunities present themselves, I'm not one to turn away.

So, we gave the network two more stories than originally planned—which likely meant little to the bosses sitting in a faraway newsroom, but not to me. It was about giving the location its due no matter what my interior state of mind might have been. We didn't have a bureau in the country, so my colleague and I aimed to make the most of the time we had. Crafting pieces as best we could to show viewers a more substantial picture of Mongolia, beyond its reputation as the Land of Eternal Sky. This meant filing reports ranging from urban pollution, poverty, and alcoholism to the dangers of mining, the triumphs of child acrobats, and the struggles of nomadic herdsmen.

Even in the dead of winter—or perhaps because of it—this was a country alive with colour.

Chinggis Khan's Kin

On one of the most vivid mornings, we found ourselves on a snow-covered steppe, as far and wide as the eye could see, with a group of traditionally dressed Mongolians dancing and chanting around a tall pyre. They claimed to be descendants of the great Mongol conqueror Chinggis Khan, and they called on his spirit by leaping around like vibrant Skittles. Tiny bursts of colour bouncing against a deep white canvas. It was other worldly.

But it was also characteristic of the certainty Mongolians have in their identity.

Despite being sandwiched between two of the world's giants—China and Russia—Mongolians proudly inhabit their distinct culture. They wear their customary colourful tunics in daily life and hold on to their ancient traditions and beliefs without question.

There's just over three million people in a country six times bigger than the UK. London alone has thrice that population. The low resident count has been put down to how difficult life is in Mongolia, where there are only harsh deserts or mountainous terrain.

Outside of Ulaanbaatar—or UB as it's often shortened—there's only steppe. Wide, endless plains. Where nomadic tribes still roam and tend to their flock. And when you are there, it is easy to feel like there is nothing else in the world but that.

We met one such roving family, headed by a jovial man named Engkee. He readily spoke to us about the challenges of keeping his herd and children fed through the winter, smiling the entire time. Indicating an acceptance of his lot. He was still better off than many others—he shared—with enough horses for his son to offer a potential bride as dowry.

And even when he didn't understand what was being said, Engkee smiled. His warm eyes disappearing into generous flush-red cheeks.

He very graciously gave me a huge block of cheese made from yak's lard and insisted we sit with the family in the ger to enjoy some tea with mare's milk. I can't say it's a beverage I would yearn for—simultaneously bitter and sour—but I was grateful for the heat inside their home. It was below freezing outside. Not counting the wind chill factor.

Made of animal skin and pelt over a latticed wood frame, the round tent ger is sturdier than it looks. Built to withstand constant gales, with interiors that are surprisingly warm and cosy. At its core sits a coal-fired stove. Families cook on it and use it for heat. Its chimney rises through a hole in the ger's crown, which can be covered during extremely bad weather.

Beds were lined along one side of Engkee's circular home, and on the other, cushions were laid around a small table.

We were welcomed like long lost friends, and the family insisted we sit for a meal. I learnt early on that saying no on occasions like this is considered rude. You must accept whatever is generously offered.

I don't recall what we were fed, but I remember the warmth in that kaleidoscope ger. It was a stellar morning with a lot of laughter and conversation, despite us not speaking the same language. Our local producer, an amiable man named Ganbat, was rather pleased we didn't rush through our visit with the herdsman's family.

At one point during the meal, as I was seated with my legs crossed to the side, I felt something nudge me. I ignored it thinking it was my imagination. But the nudging went on. When I looked down, there was a small goat pushing its nose into my leg. I mean—the horses and cattle were outside in their own dwellings, but obviously—I suppose—the goat would be in the family ger. Where else to put the thin, hairless animal in the harsh steppe winter?

It should not have, but it did surprise me to see the goat so close to where we were supping. I still recall how expectantly it looked at me, waiting for sustenance. I suspected that when it was time, this animal would also provide sustenance to its caretakers.

But it wasn't that time yet. So, I fed the goat what I could and watched as it made its way to rest at the foot of the family's heirloom chest of drawers. The beautifully decorated cabinet had been handed down through generations, and they took it with them wherever they roamed.

I felt so full by the time we left that family. And I am not referring to the food that was shared.

That morning with Engkee, I learnt that when it's cold out, that which matters or is in need of care stays in the ger.

No Ger, No Problem

Undeniably, the biting temperatures were a significant aspect of this assignment. The sun shone bright every morning, but it was still sooooo cold that my jaw would freeze, and I could barely speak to deliver a piece to camera. My face was so numb I couldn't control it.

We travelled in a heated car of course, but when we jumped out to film, the camera would frost over—and the videographer struggled to feel his fingers. We had to laugh really, but even that was difficult! Outdoors, our jaws were pretty much immobile.

Returning to our Russian-style hotel after a day of filming offered little respite. The place had a central inferno. I would say central *heating*, but it was way beyond that. It was so hot inside the hotel that I could barely breathe. And as the temperature was centralized, there was no way to decrease the heat in my room. Not even a switch to turn off the thermostat.

I confess that like an annoying tourist, I rang the front desk to ask for help. (Who can sleep in a sauna?) Bless them, the only solution they could suggest was that I pry open a window.

So, I did. Grateful for the crisp -30° C air to nip into my room. Except that within a few minutes, the room was so filled with smoke I was surprised it didn't set off an alarm. Instantly, I smelled like chargrilled barbecue from all the coal-fires being burnt in the city. UB was choked in smog. And there I was, Miss Idiot Reporter, suffocating herself indoors with smoke pollution because it was 'too hot'.

I rang the desk again and begged for another suggestion. It came moments later in the form of an electric fan. So old it must've been a remnant from the Soviet era. I don't know where exactly they found it—but I am certain I was the only person in UB sleeping with a fan in the middle of winter!

Temperature Rising

No surprise then when I eventually got sick. Again, bless the front desk, I had tried without luck to find an open pharmacy, so they jumped in and told me they would handle it.

Within minutes, I opened the door not to a packet of the expected paracetamol or acetaminophen, but a hot mug of buckthorn berry tea. It was quite an arresting yellow-orange colour. Apparently, a traditional remedy for the flu. I'd never had it before. I had also never tasted anything like it.

Did it cure me? I can't say. But it soothed my throat and certainly seemed to help. My fever broke, and I was back out filming the next day.

I never did get that bottle of Tylenol, but the hotel staff kept me on buckthorn tea the remainder of our stay. Regardless of my requesting it.

The Man

As I said earlier, on assignments like this, international journalists are lost without the aid and guidance of the local producers. And I will forever be grateful for Ganbat.

We were about the same age, and he spoke of his country like it was the most magical place on Earth. He knew its history and was abreast with all the latest news. He could speak Russian and learnt English from watching TV. He also told me about his time studying in the US. He was glad for the experience, he said, but he was so happy to return home.

Ganbat broke the stereotype expectation that people from less developed countries would rather be in more developed ones. The mere thought of migrating from Mongolia baffled him. He paused a moment to gaze at the landscape: 'Why would I ever want to leave all of this?'

Ganbat spoke with a gentle conviction about the breadth of space that pulsed beneath their Eternal Sky.

'You see this?' he stretched his arm to the vast open winter wildness. 'It is full of the spirits of creation.'

Ganbat explained that as far as Mongolian tradition is concerned, there is no such thing as empty space. Everything holds an echo of what was there before.

He spoke of his ancestors and their beliefs surrounding mortality. How death was not to be feared but celebrated. For a loved one's spirit was finally set free from this mortal coil.

We were standing by an *ovoo* when he first told me these stories. I'd never heard that word before: ovoo. They're these heaps of stones that Mongolians consider sacred. I had noticed them scattered along the scenery on our drives.

Some of the ovoos had a stick with a piece of cloth, like a flag, planted in its centre. And usually, the cloth was the colour of the sky.

Ovoos are altars or shrines, which according to Ganbat, go as far back as the days of Chinggis Khan. When going off to battle, warriors would pray together for victory, leaving stones in a pile as signs that they were there. Those who survived the conflicts came back to retrieve their markers. Any stones that remained meant those that laid them had died. That's also how they kept track of casualties.

Centuries later, Mongolians still mark passage and the loss of loved ones by leaving stones in a heap on any elevated surface. That way, their prayers are closer to the sky.

Every stone added to an ovoo represents a soul. Who may or no longer exists on the physical plane.

'So, you see,' Ganbat said, 'there are spirits everywhere, and every space there is … is occupied.'

He picked up a stone from the ground and handed it to me for my mother.

In silence, I walked around the ovoo behind him, then left a piece of my grief on that sacred heap under Mongolia's bright blue sky.

* * *

There was a full moon on our last night in the country.

Wanting to see it over the wintry landscape, we went for a drive beyond Ulaanbaatar to try and find an unobstructed stretch of evening sky.

But no matter the distance from the city, we couldn't get far enough from its light pollution. Ganbat seemed prepared to keep going, determined to show me the lunar radiance against a dark night sky. But it was getting late, and we had an early flight out the next day—so we asked the driver to just pull off the road anywhere he could.

We stopped by a snowbank that glowed a putrid gold from the urban haze.

Ganbat and I stepped out of the car with him still regaling me with stories about his ancestors.

Then, as the evening's profound cold took over, Ganbat stepped away and left me alone with the silence. In the deep bronze mist, there was only me, my wordless thoughts, and my grief.

I was left alone with the fullness of the space. It was as if every cell within me began to wake.

For the first time that I can remember, I stood bereft yet felt the cradling comfort of the universe. And I was suddenly aware that I was not alone—because I was surrounded by the presence of everything I thought I'd ever lost.

Then, in the chilling blur of that Mongolian winter's evening, I was unexpectedly engulfed by a profound sense of peace.

For the first time, I understood what Ganbat meant when he said that nothing was empty—and I realized then that **no matter what, everything's okay**.

After decades as a travelling journalist seeing the worst of humanity, I no longer felt the need to go in search of balm, because I realized it would always be there—if I stood still in the sacredness of creation.

And when I needed strength and comfort in times of chaos, I was reminded that all I had to do was turn within, where—like Engkee's goat in the ger—it would be laying silently, waiting to sustain me.

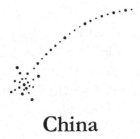

China

THERE ARE NO FALLING ~~STARS~~ IN CHINA.

It may often feel like there are as many people in China as there are stars in the heavens. But under communist rule, instead of relishing diversity, the most populous country in the world wants to engulf you in its homogeny.

Beyond its borders, few might view the behemoth through gentle eyes. But when you're known for bullying the little guys, it's not easy to see your good side.

By my first actual posting to Beijing, I had been covering China for a few years as a travelling correspondent for Al Jazeera. In 2012, the network's China-based reporter was famously thrown out for stories *displeasing* to the government—and that's when I was tapped in.

But the displeased government would not give us new work visas—so, I covered China ... from Hong Kong.

Which was lovely.

And not anything like working in the mainland.

Hong Kong was still more *itself* back then—a former British colony disposed to democracy. More liberally *Western* than subsumed into the standardized system of Chinese Communism. The dichotomy eventually led to difficulties for trapped Hong Kong.

But back then, we were free to report from the city without courting the ire of the mainland government. I could do live shots from Hong Kong on China and not worry about being ejected.

Of course, we were still getting first-hand information from Beijing. The network maintained its office there, with a producer and a cameraman.

Every day, we'd speak on the phone as the team went out to newsgather. Afterwards, they would send me the files online so I could view the material and write a script. I'd record the voiceover in Hong Kong, which would then be sent to Beijing so the team could put together the final report. They were great about keeping me in the loop and sending files back and forth, so I at least felt part of the exercise. Virtual teamwork. Reporting via remote control. But they managed to make me feel so involved that when I now view some of the stories that we filed this way, I struggle to recall if I was actually there when it was filmed.

After a productive period of working like this, I was issued a Chinese visa. Allowed to stay for a month at a time. So, it was *in* for thirty days, then back to Hong Kong until the visa was renewed.

Grey

I struggle to recall what the Chinese capital looked like. Other than the Forbidden City—which I visited on a rare clear day—all my memories are in a chokehold of grey.

I was there at the height of China's pollution issues. Readings for Beijing had air quality so bad it was fifty times higher than recommended safety levels. The crew suggested I not walk to work since, being 'new to the city', I might not be able to cope with the smog. Face mask with air filter notwithstanding. And to think, the office was barely two minutes away from where I was staying.

They were right though. If you looked out the window, you would literally see nothing. And that *nothing* was opaque. A heavy, dense veil of asphalt grey. It blocked out the sun, and in the evenings, the city lights didn't stand a chance. It could make you feel trapped in a teeny-tiny box. It was suffocating—and itchy. If you stepped out into that cack, your skin could break out in a rash, it would be near impossible to breathe without getting all sorts of crap into your lungs, and your face would inevitably be a different colour within minutes. No exaggeration. It astounded me that millions of city residents just accepted this as normal. Surely, I thought, if anything would stir discontent and make them cast anger at their government, it would be the inability to BREATHE—but a local producer maintained that so long as they could feed their families, the Chinese were used to just doing what they were told. He was adamant that nothing short of a miracle would prompt a revolution.

Neither Black nor White

Being in China was always … interesting. I'd not really worked in a place before where information was so controlled and intimidation such a part of daily life that you took it for granted. You were never sure why a source was talking, so I took everything with a grain of salt. (A pro tip for anywhere really.)

When we went to the fishing towns or far-flung villages, a government minder always seemed to appear out of thin air. Casually making their presence known to those we were speaking to. These *observers* were always someone already in the community—who'd spot our presence and follow along as we tried to work. Usually, it was a chap with a cigarette in hand, wearing an oversized black jacket, even when it wasn't cold. But then again, many of the men in the villages fit that description …

When we could, we moved around the country in pursuit of stories. I truly wish I kept a diary of those days. The places all blur into one—but as with every cosmos, there were a few bright stars that I'll always remember.

Mama Kong

None more so than Mama Kong. A sixty-five-year-old, four-foot-nothing powerhouse whose face beamed brighter than the sun. She radiated more warmth than the dank drab day over Shanxi Province. Which is where we met her.

Shanxi was among China's largest coal producers and one of the most polluted communities in the world. But this was not quite why we were there.

In defiance of China's one-child policy, Kong Zhenlan—whom everyone called Mama—had thirty-nine children in her care. Only four of them were hers biologically, which in itself was quite astounding. The others had been abandoned by their birth parents.

'I found the first one by the side of the road,' Mama Kong told us. 'How could I do nothing?'

All the children she'd taken in faced either physical or mental challenges. In China, those were seen as 'deficiencies', a reason for families to be ashamed. (I tell you, I often wonder if shame has done more damage to society than the plague.)

Studies found that many of Shanxi's 'defective' children were born as they were because of acute pollution. Toxins from burning coal and chemicals seeped into the groundwater, increasing the risk of birthing children with special needs by 450 per cent. Four-hundred-and-fifty per cent!

The children in Mama Kong's care had cleft palates, neural tube problems, brain issues, or missing—and in some instances, extra—appendages. It cost a lot to tend to them, so Mama Kong took on all sorts of jobs to earn a wage. The government had long confiscated her farmland for violating the birth control law.

That failed to faze the deeply religious Mama Kong. Word about her spread and donations poured in for the children.

By the sheer force of her will, she even managed to convince the local government to issue legal documents for some of the children, just so they could get an education.

'There is still kindness in the world,' Mama Kong grinned.

In the coal grey of the Shanxi afternoon—enveloped by the relentless grime of modern living—Mama Kong's optimism broke through the fetters of despair. Apathetic to the man in a black jacket skulking in the corner, a cigarette dangling in his hand.

A Bowl of Noodles

I was in China the last time my mother was alive on my birthday. She was an ocean away while I was down for another long, homogenous month of work. I don't recall what news there was then or what stories we covered—it's dissipated into vacuous memory.

My father had died by then, irrevocably changing the landscape of our lives. (Yes, like everyone else, sometimes, a journalist's personal life can bleed into our professional spaces.)

I recall sitting on a stool in front of a small food stall in Beijing. It was off to the side of the Forbidden City. I was nursing a tepid, watered-down coffee and a tasteless bowl of instant noodles. For long life and all that traditional Chinese birthday stuff.

There was one shrimp in the bowl. It was the only colour in an otherwise dismal dish. I had never felt so desolate.

It was a strange feeling.

My mother kept me company as I tried to eat. I rang her just to chit-chat. It's the clearest memory I have of ever doing that. Ringing my mother just to chat. I could hear the sadness in her voice—an instinctive sorrow because she knew her daughter was struggling.

I had no words for it then. The melancholy. I was just suffocating in grey and miserable. For someone who's always been fine on her own—it was a new sensation. But I had been on the road for months, working, and I was exhausted. Somewhere along the way, I had forgotten to pause for breath. So, I sat there, a solitary figure huddled against the cold on a dirty sidewalk, sipping stale coffee and flat soup, while an unintelligible world whirled all around.

I held on to my mother's voice then like a lifeline.

She was my lifeline.

And not long after that call, she was gone.

From then on, every crowded corner of China—a place she'd never been— reverberated with her overwhelming absence.

Though I'm not sure she would have appreciated the association.

Family

Having strong ties to family is often regarded as an Eastern phenomenon. Those in the geographical West somehow meant to be immune to such sentimental shackles.

When my mother was rushed to the hospital, I was expected to work—despite being owed a ton of days off. My North American line manager refused to grant my leave request, putting it thus: We all have parents who die.

I have told this story in writing once before—and I repeat it here because I am still stunned by the callousness. Anyone who would say such a thing lacks the empathy required to work in news.

Because ultimately, it is all about people. And seeing them as kin.

Sun City

As cold as China might seem, family ties are an undeniable aspect of life there.

So, when a privatized community for the elderly was built near the capital, it only added to an evolving discussion around children's obligations to their parents.

The rather swishy complex was called Sun City. And only those with means could afford to check their elderly into the purpose-built community. Some of the residents told us they felt a tad abandoned by their children, but those running the complex managed to reframe what was an uncomfortable new reality into something practical. And that holds sway in China. As it was becoming harder for families to care for their elderly, it was more *efficient* for the elderly to stay at Sun City. They would receive proper care and not run the risk of being forgotten. In other words, with the old folks in a care home, their hard-working children could keep earning for their keep, in fulfilment—not neglect—of their filial obligation. Perspective. Or propaganda? The most benevolent of spins—if you asked some of Sun City's residents.

As you would imagine, there were so many stories out of China that could be told from all sorts of perspectives. That might even give outsiders a very different view of the country. But not everyone wanted to—or could—speak. And that spoke volumes.

Among those who could, we met a lesbian activist who was detained for merely *planning* a demonstration. An amateur radio enthusiast whose hobby had him travelling to disputed waters to visit a rock claimed by China, the Philippines, and Taiwan. He wanted all sides to find a way to better communicate.

And then, there was a tiny rural community whose elderly were dying of illness brought on by acute air pollution.

So many small voices. Easy to miss in the swelling breadth of China's insistent, one-note opera.

In that homogenous smog, how do we know what we are looking at?

And what is the truth?

One Note

One night, my colleagues and I were flying back to Beijing from some town or other—I no longer knew where we were and was rather lost in a fog of my own. We were seated in the middle row, and I had the video monitor switched onto a live feed of the plane's 'sky cam'. The night outside was inky black. Or the camera wasn't on. Which could very well have been the case.

But then, suddenly, a streak of white across the dark. A falling star!

Always one to make a wish, I saw it as a good sign.

I shared this news excitedly with my colleague flipping through the local papers beside me.

'There are no falling stars in China,' he dismissed. Without even glancing up from the page.

I ignored his derision and proposed that he may have thought that because he didn't bother to look.

He laughed at my naïveté. Insisting he didn't have to look to know. As if such an image was beyond any Chinese reality, which was always obscured by *smog*.

The way he and many others saw it: life in the modern incarnation of the Middle Kingdom was just something to be endured. There couldn't possibly be space in it for something as *wondrous* as a falling star.

He was so accepting of things as they were that he wouldn't even consider otherwise.

Maybe I should have referred to it in science-speak—as a meteor. And reminded him that smog eventually dissipates.

This colleague was the same one who taught me how to breathe through the haze, and where to walk to avoid the dregs. He pointed out what not to eat and what not to trust. It was a cultural as well as an interpersonal exchange. He was learning Spanish, and often spoke of his plans for a future that did not involve Beijing. (He may not have realized it, but he too was wishing on unseen stars.)

We had also just met a merchant, a rural boy turned successful exporter of sweaters to Israel. He was investing all his earnings to create a life in New Zealand for his children. He was saving up to send them to university and bought them a house in Auckland. A place he'd never been.

'I hear there are big trees there,' he shared shyly, 'and nice open spaces …'

He just wanted to give his family the chance to breathe unobstructed. 'Is it true you can always see the sky, there?'

The awe on his face when we assented was almost as stunning as Mama Kong.

Something in the Air

One morning, before dawn had broken, this same colleague came to pick me up on our way to the airport for another domestic trip. He was almost exuberant.

'Guess what,' he grinned. 'I took a chance when I woke up and looked out my window'—he paused waiting for me to ask—'just like you said, I saw one.'

I thought I knew where this was headed but I didn't want to presume.

'A shooting star!' he exclaimed assuredly. 'I looked and saw a shooting star!'

It made his day.

This may seem like a small matter in the grander scheme, but we should hold on to the bits of stardust that keep us hopeful.

Falling star, shooting star, meteor—whatever you might call it, **the light is there.**

And even in China, that which conceals things will clear—and those on the ground will reflect the stars above.

NORTH AMERICA

California

HOLLYWOOD IS A STATE OF MIND.

As an Al Jazeera correspondent assigned to cover Asia, I never expected to report from California.

Technically, I was on the Asia *Pacific* beat—and though it is some 7,000 miles away—California does face the Pacific Ocean, so in a sense I suppose that fits, right?

Well, not according to my news manager—whom I tried (but failed) to convince to send me to cover the Oscars. Bah-humbug.

Anyway, I may not have made it to the globally known, star-studded showbiz awards show, but I was sent to California, nonetheless. Thanks to then US president Barack Obama and his bannered 'pivot' to Asia.

In line with that geopolitical strategy, in February 2016, Obama hosted the first ever Stateside summit between the US and the Association of Southeast Asian Nations (ASEAN). Their reinforced 'partnership' an important milestone in the face of China's growing influence—and belligerence—in the Pacific.

So, off to Los Angeles I went.

For work.

'Bad Trip'

For me, the US is a place of nostalgia and mixed emotions. I was eight years old the first time I visited—and I didn't want to be there.

Italy was my preferred destination. I had just done an oral presentation on the country for history class and really really *really* wanted to see Rome.

There's No Place Like Rome

Yes, I was an odd little child obsessed with Caesar and the Colosseum. My father was none too pleased. He had saved up and planned a whole North American adventure for the summer. It started in Vancouver and included a drive down the Pacific Coast Highway from the Golden Gate bridge in San Francisco to the San Diego Zoo.

Plus, there was going to be a visit to the wondrous magical kingdom of Disneyland.

Every child's dream, right?

Except this child—ignorant of costs and budgets—wanted to see the Pope in the Vatican, not Mickey Mouse in California.

Fool's Holiday

So, I sulked. For much of the trip.

Like a total idiot.

(Yes, I know I was a pain.)

It must be said that there are photos of me with a hint of a smile posing with Chip 'n' Dale—no, not furniture nor the troupe of erotic male dancers, but Disney's giant chipmunk mascots. Proof that I must've enjoyed the visit—despite myself.

There is also a picture of me with my parents at San Francisco's Pier 39. I am sitting on my father's lap, captured in a fit of laughter. He was tickling me so I might look happy for the camera.

And I did look happy.

I *was* happy.

Despite myself.

Aside from the memories conjured by those photos, there is one thing that stands out from that trip that wasn't captured by our instamatic camera. It couldn't have been.

My father drove me up and down Doheny Drive in Los Angeles, until I was ready for him to stop.

Driving Doheny

What was on West Hollywood's Doheny Drive? The only thing that I thought I wanted to see in the US—I had read in a fan magazine that this was where John Travolta lived.

Besides Italy, this eight-year-old was obsessed with the Italian American actor. Go figure.

It had nothing to do with John Travolta being of Italian descent. I just loved the way he danced in *Saturday Night Fever*—although I was too young then to understand the film. (I still get goose bumps watching clips.)

And—of course—like the rest of the world, I adored him in *Grease*.

The Christmas before that US trip with my parents, the Three Kings (also my parents, as I later found out) gave me the best gift ever. Underneath my small shoe, which—as Christmas tradition dictated—I put out by our front door, the 'Wise Men' left a giant poster of John Travolta. It was already mounted and set to hang in my room.

It was autographed, too. (Again, I found out later that it was, of course, a mass-produced copy. But no matter.)

That Gift of the Magi made my year. (Almost as much as a trip to Rome might have.)

In Search of Travolta

Anyway—so, there we were in Los Angeles on a trip of a lifetime and my father patiently drove his irritatingly sulky eight-year-old up and down Doheny Drive trying to look for an address that didn't exist.

This is why after all the driving holidays my father later took us on (including—finally—a trip to Rome), this first one remains the most special.

Because it taught me that often, the best parts of a journey are the things you find when you're not looking.

Driving Lessons

When I wasn't moping about *not* being in Rome, I found I liked seeing the ocean from the back seat window of our rented station wagon.

I enjoyed discovering new places I hadn't written school reports about nor even knew existed.

Interesting places like a small Dutch town in California, numerous Spanish missions along the Pacific, and magical redwood forests just steps from a beach.

I was happy to explore city gardens and fruit orchards and try fabled fare at iconic stops like Pea Soup Andersen's.

Many times since, I have found myself in other places I did not want to be. But I no longer struggled against it.

I had learnt when I was eight that it does no good to box yourself up in frustrated expectations.

Baby, You Can Drive My Car

After my father died, I drove myself along the California coast retracing the journey he first took me on.

I understood then why he loved to take the family on long drives: there is a meditativeness to being behind the wheel.

I stopped at the places he introduced me to—and every day, watched the sun set on the crashing ocean.

At many points along the way, I cried like a child.

Then, I treated myself to Danish pastries and pea soup.

With each mile, I gave thanks that my father was a fun-loving adventurer—who didn't stop tickling his grumpy eight-year-old until she laughed and opened herself to the unknown.

Next Stop, Hollywood

So, in 2016, I returned to California on a mission—to appreciate every second of the new reportorial terrain and look beyond its sheen of projected glamour.

The first thing that struck me was how intensely the sun shone in Los Angeles. I lived in Asia at the time, but nothing there seemed to burn as bright as the Hollywood day.

The glare in the City of Stars was unforgiving. And heavy with the opportunities left unclaimed by fearful dreamers.

In a place without shadows, there is no hiding your failings or bruises.

And it isn't easy to lift your gaze when the light can blind even in the most tucked away of corners.

So, new arrivals learn to keep their eyes behind dark lenses and ponder how they might stand out in a city bursting with the hopes of millions.

They keep their eyes shaded—and collectively choose to believe in illusions.

Take One

In LA, everywhere I looked someone was planning their hit-in-the-making one-man show, writing their soon-to-be-best-selling manuscript, or rehearsing the acceptance speech for their sure-to-come award.

As I sat in cafes reading up on the news, I realized that at every other table was a lost dreamer struggling to keep their optimism intact. A cliché of the Hollywood newbie, I know, but true.

LA is unapologetically a city of clichés. And if you stay put for even a moment, you'll spot them.

The yoga addict carrying her rolled-up, neon-coloured, mat confidently under her arm.

The bleach-haired hipster in overalls and gold sneakers.

The skinny model-wannabe in a sequined t-shirt and barely-there, skimpy, jean shorts.

The overly built, perfectly coiffed muscle man in the too-tight, pastel-coloured shirt, Bluetooth buds securely in his ears as he gazes with steely intensity into the distance.

The lady-who-lunches striding by with carefully choreographed nonchalance; her pedicured feet stop and do an about-turn as she decides to stop for a mug of cold brew coffee or matcha with almond milk at three in the afternoon.

Then, of course, there's the loud poser who whips along making declarations into his mobile as if he has swallowed a megaphone. He is very important. That's what he wants everyone around him to think, as he talks inconsequential nonsense at someone on the other end of the line.

This was my typical weekday in Los Angeles, where if people weren't plying each other with bullshit, they stared off into space trying to conquer self-aggrandised demons.

There was a certain absurdity to this life of 'dreams'.

Take Two

One bright morning—working with a chiselled, sun-tanned LA crew—I found myself filming pieces-to-camera on Santa Monica Beach, the boardwalk, and around Chinatown. Tourist attractions that were going into building a political news report.

For someone used to less *scenic* locations, it was quite a change.

Days later, I drove myself some two hundred kilometres inland from LA to the desert in Rancho Mirage, where the US-ASEAN summit was to take place in an historic estate called Sunnylands. The two-hundred-acre property sits between Frank Sinatra and Bob Hope Drives, and is considered a modern architectural marvel.

Once a private home, the stunning setting went on to host 'high-powered' retreats for political leaders and opened its doors for educational and arts purposes.

Nothing extraordinary came out of that US-ASEAN summit, but those involved declared it a success. And I was glad for the chance to report from Sunnylands.

But other than that site and the gorgeous desert sunsets, again what I recall most about being in California wasn't captured by the camera.

Me Llamo Rogelio

He was riffling through the trash bins of the place I was staying at when I spotted him. A shadowy figure in broad daylight.

Slowly, he turned and looked at me like a cat caught hunting for prey. His weather-beaten face expressionless. No shame. No anger. No sadness. Nothing.

For a few moments, our eyes locked, then he resumed riffling through the bins.

I let him be and went inside, thinking to get him some food.

When I came back out, he was done foraging and was sitting on the pavement.

I handed him a sandwich and joined him.

Rogelio was forty-three-years-old. His Latin movie star name was contradicted by his untamed beard, tattered baseball cap, and threadbare clothes.

Next to him sat a shopping trolley full of plastic bottles, glass, bits of wood, and paper. Anything he could sell for recycling.

Like a shared secret, Rogelio told me openly that he crossed into the US on foot from Mexico. Through Texas, just three months prior.

He thought I was Colombian. I corrected him, but it didn't seem to matter. Since I had stopped to speak to him—in his language—he was happy to talk.

I learnt that in California, particularly in Los Angeles, the Spanish language creates a strong sense of camaraderie. And almost inevitably, makes you part of a different layer of LA society. A sector mostly overlooked.

But anywhere in the world really, people 'abroad' who speak a shared language often help each other out. And for the most part, they keep each other's secrets.

City of Secrets

So, Rogelio went on and told me it wasn't his first time to walk across the border from Mexico into the States.

'But it has been getting harder,' he added.

He did odd jobs in Texas to pay for his way to California. Always his ultimate destination.

Why LA? 'Because there's loads of money here,' Rogelio stated, 'so, there will be jobs.'

Another dreamer in the City of Dreams. But that was the extent of his: to earn money. To find work.

'Anything, really. I can tend gardens. Work outdoors, that kind of thing—' he trailed off.

Rogelio appeared to prefer to work alone so he wouldn't have to speak. He didn't know English and stayed away from people who did.

But regardless of language—and the punishing state of his day-to-day—he was confident that in LA there were opportunities.

'Merloss'

When I met him, *home*, for Rogelio, was one of the many cardboard camps along the side-streets of 'Merloss'. His word for Melrose Avenue. The bustling commercial lifeline that courses through the heart of LA's Hollywood neighbourhood.

He slept—when he could—under blaring neon lights and the iconic HOLLYWOOD sign. Just one of almost sixty thousand people then without permanent homes in Los Angeles County.

Their numbers were on the rise. Only New York—which has a larger population in general—had more people without homes. Most of them were African American. Latinos, like Rogelio, were next. And there was a growing number of military veterans living on the streets, pushed out of the housing market by sky-rocketing prices.

Trolley

Rogelio wasn't sure how long he would stay in LA. He said that if he didn't find work, he would likely return to Mexico. At least, for a little bit.

I remained silent, unsure what to say.

He then asked if I had 'papers' or perhaps entered the States the same way he had.

He looked wistful when I told him I was only visiting.

'How nice,' he surmised, 'to be able to do that.'

We sat, again, in silence.

After a little while: 'Can you work a cash register? There are a few places in Merloss that have jobs going. You might want to check them out.'

Like a co-conspirator, he wanted to help. 'There are opportunities,' he repeated, 'if you know where to look.'

I thanked him. And assured him that I was ok and would soon be leaving the country.

Rogelio smiled warmly, wringing together his rough, stained hands.

Then, slowly, he rose from the pavement.

'You take care now,' he said, softly. Without a backward glance.

Illusion

Like most things in Hollywood, Rogelio was deceptive in his appearance.

On first sight, his blank stare and unkempt countenance may have given off the illusion of defeat, but as he walked away—pushing in front of him his cart full of plastic and cardboard—Rogelio went unbowed, a hopeful realist bent on pursuing his dreams.

For some reason, this brought me back to the sulking child in the backseat of her father's rented station wagon. Whose world broke open as she begrudgingly watched California's Pacific Coastline whizz by. On that family trip, I learnt that **unfathomable treasures lie just beyond our limitations**—if we let go of what blinds us and holds us back.

All these years later, a life on the road has shown me that we are each on deeply personal journeys—in pursuit of dreams we may fear will not come true. But no matter the challenges or the state of one's reality, as demonstrated by Rogelio, **it doesn't cost to be kind**. He tried to help me get work when he himself was hungry, without the need to compete or feel a sense of lack.

He shone bright with generosity and optimism, even in the unforgiving blaze of the Hollywood sun.

SOUTH AMERICA

Brazil

IT'S BEST TO WALK THE BEACH WHEN YOU'RE COLOURBLIND.

For me, Brazil is a burst of citrus cutting through a heavy bog. Fresh, tart colours highlighting the complex shades of luscious foliage.

It has a taste too, Brazil. The bold acidic density of coffee sharpened by bright rays of lime.

Music aficionados will be familiar with its sound—the ruffling of a pregnant breeze against the seductive rhythm of voluptuous rain.

They call it bossa nova.

In February 2016, US President Obama hosted the leaders of Southeast Asian countries in California for the first stateside American-Pacific conference. I was in LA to cover that, then sent on to Brazil in the run-up to the Olympics.

The games were going to be held in the famed beach city Rio de Janeiro, which was later recognized a UNESCO World Heritage site for its 'exceptional' urban setting. Where the stunning natural landscape was so fused to the local culture that it was deemed an 'outdoor living' city like no other.

Rio developed on a narrow strip of land between the Atlantic Ocean and Guanabara Bay, overlooked by rolling hills and steep forested peaks.

So, it was the start of summer—it was Rio—it certainly sounded like a *joyful* posting.

Here's the But

But with only weeks to go until the games, Brazil faced a major health emergency while simultaneously grappling with an astonishing political crisis. The mosquito-borne Zika virus was thought[2] to be causing birth abnormalities, and the country's biggest ever case of political corruption was unfurling like a tempest.

Talk about *when it rains* …

Waters of March

When I recall Brazil,
    the memories   don't flood back   in images   or words,
    but in
                emotions.
They tip t o e in like   ten t a t iv e
                       rain.
Coy
          and   light.
    Drop.
        By
          drop.

---

2 Nearly a decade later, no causality had yet been established between the Zika virus and microcephaly in Brazilian new-borns. Cases were confined to a small area in the country's northeast, and numbers dropped in the first year.

Playfully tugging   at   my heart   as   f in ger t i p s
                                                    a new guitar.

Then, what usually begins as a strum (a shower) becomes   a chord
                                                           (a storm),

      a drizzle quicklyturnsinto

                            a down

                                  p

                                    o

                                        u

                                          r

                                                ,

            corpulent drops of rain
      prancing on sheet metal roofs like

                              l i t h   e

                  nimble fi n g e r s
                  on a baby grand.

    It is in the magical rhythm of Antonio Carlos Jobim's 'Waters
of March' that I recall Brazil.

    If you've never heard the iconic song by the legendary
composer, do yourself the favour of looking it up online. Find
the version from 1974 in which he sings with another Brazilian
legend, Elis Regina. You'll hopefully hear what I mean.

    Considered the most popular song to come out of Brazil,
Jobim wrote 'Waters of March' to mimic rain. Notes in staccato—
and images in verses—falling on your ears in celebration of the
coming spring.

    It's in March—when summer is ending—that the rains in Rio
are strongest.

    Through the chaos of Brazil in March 2016, the hypnotic
bossa nova tap-tap-tapping was soothing.

At the end of my days in Rio, I listened to the song on loop as the city's lights came on beneath the shadow of the towering Christ the Redeemer statue.

That moment of marriage between dusk and Jobim's music was a necessary sacrament of space and breath.

Operation Car Wash

In 2016, Brazil was two years into its biggest criminal investigation (which also happened to kick off in March).

Initially focused on money laundering through a car wash, the so-called Operation Car Wash lasted until 2021 and became the largest anti-graft effort in the world.

It eventually saw the indictment of over five hundred high-level politicians and businesspeople, but also led to Brazil's worst judicial scandal.

And for all its seemingly good intentions, Operation Car Wash was revealed as likely to have been used to advance rival political aims. (Surprise, surprise.)

The primary malfeasance involved contract fixing and taking kickbacks from Petrobras, the large state-owned petrol company.

The case brought down a government—headed by the country's first female president—and ultimately, nearly two hundred people were convicted.

In 2016, Operation Car Wash pretty much overshadowed a troubled Olympics, which despite the hype, came across poorly managed and staged.

In 2016, what was meant to be an economy on the rise was instead in crisis—the worst in over a hundred years. Floundering under the same ruling leftist party credited with lifting millions of people out of poverty.

So much for what I thought would be a 'joyful' assignment. Brazil seemed on the verge of imploding.

Playing Ball

In short: as newsgathering goes, it was a busy time. So, when I could, I would take breathers, which included having lunch at a place along Copacabana Beach that was near the office. It offered a buffet of local food and had views of the popular shoreline.

I didn't realize it at first, but turns out, Rio's beaches are—in a way—colour-coded.

In Brazil—as I learnt—people are defined by the hue of their skin. They're either white, black, brown, or yellow. Or various combinations thereof.

Like most other places in the world, those on the lighter end of the spectrum are at the top of the social strata.

The restaurant staff was mostly comprised of those from the opposite end.

I ate at that place enough times that those who worked there had come to expect me. And when I was the only patron around, they took turns coming over to chat. Doing so, I suppose, because I sat alone and was no different to them in hue.

Once, a new manager almost blocked me from entering to sit at my usual table, until the wait staff informed him that I was a regular. (I think my less than impressive attire may have contributed to his judgement.)

The saviour server was a man called Assis. He was from a poorer part of the country and worked long hours to support his entire extended family. (Yes, Assis and I talked quite a bit.)

But despite putting in the time—and paying his taxes—Assis still couldn't afford much and didn't reap any benefits from social services. Worse, he said, his ailing mother-in-law had been supplanted from a transplant list by someone with more money. It was the last straw.

'They think we are fools!'

Assis said that although wider society considered him 'uneducated', even he could see that corruption was endemic and politicians were making a mockery of the country.

Like many Brazilians, he felt betrayed by the ruling Workers' Party—they were supposed to be on 'the people's' side, not using the system for their own advantage.

'They're playing *papa caliente*,' Assis stated. A childhood game, he explained, popular in many parts of Brazil regardless of skin tone. Players pass a ball around with the aim of not getting caught with it when the music stops. Whoever's left holding the ball is out.

'That's what the politicians are doing,' Assis said, disgusted. 'None of them want to get caught with the ball. They're all pointing fingers, investigating each other, and revealing secrets … it's ridiculous.'

Assis hated being judged and limited by the prejudices against the shade of his skin. He may not have received a formal education, but he told me that he learnt what he could and taught himself to speak five languages.

He wanted to be heard and recognized as no less significant than anyone else in the country.

It was only the need to earn that kept him from joining the growing street protests calling for the government's ouster. The paler middle classes could *afford* to skip work, he said—with only a tinge of resentment at how keen they seemed to put the blame for corruption on the leaders of the Workers' Party.

Covering the story took us from Rio to the halls of power in the purpose-built capital, Brasilia, then to São Paulo, the country's largest metropolis. Each city had its own distinct vibe, but in all, there was a rising anger at their leaders. Ultimately, the corruption scandal crossed political lines, and encompassed all shades of Brazilian society.

End Game

When back in Rio and at the end of what were very colourful workdays, I would go for unhurried walks along the curves of

Copacabana's iconic black-and-white promenade, until the four-kilometre beach turned into Ipanema and the quieter Leblon, to watch dusk drape itself over the Two Brothers Mountains. The unmistakable silhouette rose in the distance like conjoined sharks between sky and sea.

Eventually, I began to spot the sections of beach that seemed almost reserved for use by certain sectors of society.

Tanner locals played football and hung out in one area, while younger, more moneyed people mingled and had their cocktails in another.

There were ambulant vendors selling beers and juices, and other merchants showcasing their wares on towels spread out over the sand.

Among them, tourists roamed blissfully unaware of the social mores that corrupted Rio's free communal pastime—going to the beach.

Her Name is Rio

Regardless of social and political strife, Rio de Janeiro pulsated with life. Even when the skies threatened rain.

Most representative of the city's buzz were the hive-like communities cascading down the mountainsides, just feet from the sea. Rio was full of them. The colourful *favelas*—with their winding alleys and narrow, vertigo-inducing homes—stood as testament to the deep racism often glossed over in favour of the image of Brazilians as easy-going, carnival-hosting revellers who chill to bossa nova with caipirinhas.

Ironically, the favelas—where Rio's poorest live—have the best view of the sea. Outsiders are warned to never visit unless invited and then only go with protection.

Despite their central presence, favela residents are undeniably marginalized and underprivileged.

And most of them are Black.

Black Brazil

Of Brazil's two hundred million people, majority are of African descent. A legacy of the colonial slave trade—which the country only abolished in 1888, the last in the Americas to do so.

White Brazilians earn nearly fifty per cent more than this majority—and that inequality bleeds into every aspect of life.

As of this writing, in Brazil[3]:

- a Black man dies every 23 minutes
- 75 per cent of people murdered are Black
- police are behind most of those killings
- 91 per cent of those killed by stray bullets are Black children

Racism is so ingrained in the fabric of life that many Brazilians will tell you it's institutional.

Just like corruption.

Back to the Suds

With Operation Car Wash turning up revelation after revelation, we were reporting live practically every hour.

And every hour, there were so many new developments it could give you whiplash.

Our Brazilian producer said he always worried about having to explain all the intricacies of domestic politics to the 'foreign' correspondents rotating in—but he felt I understood it on first hearing. This surprised him.

Truth be told, given my experience in the Philippines, it was rather easy to follow.

You see, here's what I've learnt throughout the years: Social stratification exists everywhere, and corruption is corruption—no matter who is behind it or how.

---

3 The following figures are from Ciara Nugent and Thaís Regina, 'How Black Brazilians are looking to a slavery-era form of resistance to fight injustice today', *Time*, 16 December 2020; also see, the Brazilian NGO, Coalizaõ Negra Por Direitos.

Weak, self-serving politicians are not exclusive to Latin America or developing countries—they're found anywhere there is power and money to be grabbed. And it isn't difficult to spot the perpetrators.

As for the challenges brought about by skin tone, that too is not limited to countries in the Western hemisphere. You see it in the race for beauty bleaching products in Asian countries. Or in the booming industry of cosmetic surgery that promises taller noses, higher cheekbones, and wider eyes.

(An aside: I was not the kind of journalist who worked for accolades. I didn't go up for awards or chase nominations. I just wanted to do all I could to give every story its due, but I was never sure if I succeeded. So, when one of my live reports from Brazil was featured on a popular US news review show not as something to laugh at but as an explainer of the complex rigmarole—it made me feel like I'd done the job well. A small triumph, but it meant a lot.)

Beats

My employers asked me to re-base to Brazil in 2016. At any other point I may have jumped at the chance, but in my gut I knew the time had come for me to leave the profession. If even for a little while. It had been my whole life for the better part of some twenty-five years—and I did love it—but the pace had gotten so I needed the spaces and pauses-for-breath to be a little longer. Once you are too tired to even know where you are, it is time to stop. And believe me, I am aware of how fortunate I was to have been able to even consider such a decision.

I left Brazil before the worst unfolded, and shortly after, put away my mic and reporter's notebook.

But it all comes back to me when I hear the rain or see a sun set.

Or shut my eyes to feel the rhythm of my heart.

Rio's sunsets were the most striking when the heavens were turbulent. Before a storm, the sky took on the sheen of a black opal swirling into the depths of an indigo sea.

It was being in Brazil that reinforced the notion for me that corruption and prejudice are like the weather—affecting everyone no matter how much you might think you're protected.

When it's cold out, it's cold out regardless of the price of your coat. And in the summer, the sun will shine no matter what section of the beach you're on.

The End of the Road

On one of my last nights in Rio, the darkness was shattered by a hundred rivers of light. Like Baccarat crystal crashing on a cobalt floor.

It was the most brilliant of evenings.

In all my years covering natural calamities and climate change, I'd never seen anything like it—a dry thunderstorm. The night sky was so alive, and though cracked open, there was no rain. To think, Rio gets its heaviest downpours when it's on the cusp of spring ...

When water

falls

in d

r

o

ps

that become

cascades.

But raining or not, a storm is a storm ...

is a storm.

When darkness falls, the colours disappear—making it easier to see through a camouflaged world and find beauty.

So, while Brazil may have shown that corruption—political, social, moral—is colourblind, fortunately for us all, so is love.

THE UNITED KINGDOM

By the River Thames

London

YOU CAN JUMP EVEN WITH A BROKEN FOOT.

If there was no option but to open this collection of recollections in Manila, then *needs must* close it in London. This really isn't where it ends, but simply a curve in the river.

Living by the Thames was the manifestation of a dream I didn't even know I had. Some of my most important years were spent in the UK. It gave me a chance to evolve in ways I could not have even fathomed. Nearing a decade there, I was still not quite ready to leave—but it was time to leave the job at CNN. Management had changed and I knew I had reached a dead end. Even though I'd been with the network for almost six years.

Before the End

So, how did I get there to begin with? I have often been asked. In a nutshell, here goes: Remember in that chapter on Manila I mentioned taking a summer job to help me put funds together for that first trip to Europe? Well, it was in advertising, and through that gig, I met an executive who later gave me a lead on another summer opening in media. This time, at one of the Philippines' main TV channels. I was majoring in Communications then and the job was in their newsroom. Ideal for the obligatory college internship credits.

That summer gig turned into a full-time job once I graduated from university. After several years of working there as a reporter and news presenter, I was offered a scholarship to do a journalism masters in the UK. It took some convincing, but I was allowed to study literature instead. I really wanted to delve deeper into the art and craft of storytelling itself and how this reflected the various states of the human condition. And vice versa. How the human condition informs our storytelling. I felt this would serve to broaden and enrich how I approached the news.

I did the degree in London and absolutely fell in love with the city. Got a small room in a flat-share not far from the Thames, and walked along its banks at every opportunity. No day—and no trek—was the same. I made the most of everything the city had to offer and submerged myself in cultural experiences. Devouring books, attending talks, visiting museums, and going to the theatre.

It was hard to leave when I completed my post-grad degree. So, I found a way to stay. Took on odd jobs to finance the experience. My father was always encouraging, telling me to fearlessly go after what I wanted. I was in my twenties then and didn't even consider failure an option.

It was also the early days of the internet and people still weren't turning to Google for answers to all their questions. *Jeeves*[4] was around to *ask* but hardly as helpful as one might've needed.

---

4 Launched in 1997, Ask Jeeves was one of the first online sites offering to answer any questions it was asked. A precursor to later and more popular search engines like Google and AI chatbots. It was named after the typical English gentleman's valet, as the site intended to *fetch* answers on command. It was dissolved in 2006.

So, I remember scouring bookstores for production manuals and lists of companies that were involved in news and current affairs. I wrote letters to the ones that I thought might be open to a young reporter from halfway around the world, whose country didn't really have a colonial history with the Empire. There weren't many, so I broadened my search. I typed out my pitch and addressed envelopes by hand, then posted them in the mailbox down the street. I must've easily sent out over a hundred. Replies? Barely a handful. None of which were as enthusiastic as I had hoped. More like: Thanks, but no. Rote. And cold. But at least, they bothered to reply. The rest ghosted me before ghosting was even a thing. Did I lose heart? Yes. But for some reason, I was determined to keep going. At that point, it felt like everything was still ahead of me, and I wasn't about to turn back or give up until … well, I had no idea *until* when.

And I didn't have a back-up plan.

Every time I spoke to my parents long distance, my mother would entreat me to come home, and my father would ask if that's what I wanted to do. When I'd tell him I wasn't ready to return yet, he would reinforce his reassurance and urge me to follow my dreams—so long as I was willing to find something that would sustain me in the meantime.

'And when you just can't do it anymore,' I recall him saying, 'then you come home.'

I was so very grateful for his enthusiastic support of my pipe dream. It does indeed help knowing there's a safety net. *Going home*. But at the time, that was far from an option.

Not Going Home

For a few years after I completed my Master's, I stayed involved in TV and journalism by helping where I could on documentaries— none of it paid. It was mostly just research and support work on Filipino-related programs. Nothing that would cover the rent.

So, concurrently, I kept a (paying) clerical job, which entailed putting lots of papers in little envelopes and posting them out. Answering phones and cashier work. I also did a lot of stapling. A LOT. It was my first 'desk job', if you will.

That led to another job as an assistant in a small wine agency. A British firm that imported and distributed specialist wine from all over the world. I was PA to the chairman. A lovely old Englishman who thought me overqualified but was happy for the help. Before me, his daughter had the role, but she no longer wanted to work for Dad.

Because I was 'overqualified', they very kindly taught me the ropes of the industry, had me in meetings with business partners and designing wine lists. They also sent me to get my Wine Certification. I needed a Level 2 Certificate to officially become a company sales rep. Maybe this was the role meant for me. The track was opening. I was going to be a professional alcoholic. This was what I said to my mother—who was less than amused. My father thought it rather funny. My parents drank nothing harder than soda. But I must admit, as grateful as I was for the added knowledge and the official certificate, there was a part of me that was beginning to get bored. My life entailed walking to work at 9 a.m., opening up the office, sitting around waiting to be assigned things to do, and staring out the window. We had a lovely spot in Victoria, just behind Buckingham Palace, with a large bay window looking out onto the street. It was a fishbowl. People would walk by and see me at my desk. It was like being a living mannequin in a shop window.

The job itself was easy, predictable, and safe. 9–4. Sometimes, maybe 5. But rarely. I also became easy acquaintances with a few bar owners and restauranteurs who had establishments near where I lived. And on weekends, my flatmates and I could pop by as if visiting friends. I knew my Rieslings from my Gewürtzes, and my Shiraz from my Carménère. But I also knew this wasn't the reason I wanted to stay in London in the first place.

Then, one day I heard there was a new boss at the CNN London office. A man I had met years back in Manila. He visited the network I was working for, and I think I introduced myself to him then. I *think* I did—but I wasn't sure. It didn't matter. I found the number of the CNN office and decided to give him a ring. Before him, I had sent a letter to his predecessor—as part of that whirlwind of mail-outs—and obviously, got no response. So, I didn't want to bother with that whole post thing again, hence—a phone call.

Breaking Out of the Fishbowl

I dialled the number for CNN, asked for the bureau chief by name, and got put through directly. Just like that. I was gobsmacked. I didn't think that would work. I had no idea what to say—I didn't plan that far ahead. I truly did not think I would get through. I believe I muttered something about meeting him in Manila and wanting to see if he might have anything open in his bureau for someone with my experience. He was warm and friendly, and told me to send him my CV—score! I got his email address. That began a back and forth for about six months. At the time, he had nothing for a young reporter/presenter from the Philippines who had gotten a Master's in literature and was working in a wine company. But he told me to come around for coffee if I was ever 'in the area'. Of course, I was in the area the very next day.

We met for a quick cappuccino across the street from CNN, and he told me he would keep me 'in mind' should anything pop up. I went away buoyed for even having got that far. Of course, nothing 'popped up' but since I had his email address, I didn't think twice about keeping in touch. Dropping him an occasional line. About items I read that I thought he'd find interesting or something I saw on CNN. Other times I wrote just to say hi and remind him I was still around.

Fortunately, because he'd worked in Asia, he knew the quality of the networks then in the Philippines, which was rather good.

These were the days before everyone and everything had an online presence, so you can imagine what other people in the wider world knew about Manila and its media—zip, zilch, nada. Which could be why I wasn't getting a foot in anywhere. But thanks to this man's own experience of Southeast Asia, he wasn't so quick to dismiss.

After six months of me asking if the bureau needed an assistant or even just someone to spool tapes and do the coffee run, he asked me to come and see him. A job had come up!

'You're overqualified,' he said, 'but it's a staff position and if you want it, it's yours. It's a foot in the door, kid, and once you're in the network, how far you go is up to you.'

And that's how I landed a job at CNN. Pushing buttons, communicating to bureaus around the world, and recording video in the MCR—the master control room. I was thrilled. It was a windowless room full of screens and switches and knobs, but when it was busy with breaking news, the room buzzed with excitement just like the adrenalin-pumping scenes in my childhood favourite film, *Broadcast News*. I was sure I would one day get to the coveted position played by Holly Hunter—news producer.

In time, I was asked to pinch-hit on the newsdesk, answering calls that actually had to do with newsgathering, making plans and dealing with seasoned correspondents as they put together their reports. Occasionally, I was asked to be the weekend reporter and to help out during the week when there was a need. There were days that I would be in MCR taking in video feeds, while at the same time, writing scripts for news packages to air. I was a multi-tasker and proud of it. Training in Manila, you see. Production budgets were low, so everyone had to learn to do the job of at least five people. It was tough but came in super handy when trying to prove yourself in an international arena.

Say What Now?

Thing is, I didn't realize until much later that I had also imbibed more of a colonial mentality than I thought. And I thought

I wasn't afflicted with it at all. I remember my boss in the wine company saying he was 'rather impressed' that his PA could speak to anyone in a room, and to everyone in the same manner. Waiter, wine buyer, sommelier, executives, and vintners. It was my 'house training', I explained. My parents taught us to treat everyone the same, no one was better or lesser than you. So, the English and their social classes and foibles didn't faze me. I was, after all, not part of the British colonial hierarchy.

(Having said this, when Queen Elizabeth II came to launch the new CNN London office in 2001, I was the staff person who had to pretend to be working in the brand new but still offline, open-plan MCR. She came right to where I was and made a comment about 'all the buttons'. I admit I was rather thrilled at being in the presence of such a major figure in history. I digress ...)

Anyway, I was naïve to think that over the years, I had not internalized some racial prejudices. As much as I loved working at CNN, there was part of me that couldn't believe I was there, with my heroes. With people I had watched growing up. I kept jumping when asked, no matter how high. And I never said no, once not sleeping for three days because I thought that's what was required ... until I was told later that I could've and should've refused. I didn't know that. I never even considered it. I was not a Westerner, surely I should just be grateful for the opportunity. This notion existed within me simultaneous with the belief that I was no better or worse than anyone else. Looking back now, I can see how I basically negated my own advancement. I needed to get out of my own way—and I had not.

In the end, news management changed, and unfortunately, I was back to being just the Asian girl who worked in master control. I would have to prove myself all over again.

But by then, I had proved enough to myself ... to know that I was ready to stand on my own. I was ready to step out of the shadows and create my own path.

And to do that, I had to take the first—frightening—step.

Here We Go Again

At the time, articles began appearing in industry papers about a new English language news channel that was in the works. Revolutionarily, it would not be headquartered in the geographical West but in the Middle East. And it intended to tell more stories from overlooked parts of the world. Al Jazeera.

It already had an Arabic news channel, and thanks to living in London—and my experience in Iraq—I knew it to be a reputable network and not an extension of a terrorist organization, which is how it was portrayed by several Western nations.

As you may have realized by now, I can get dogged when I need/want to accomplish something. So, I found the names of the newly appointed executives and blindly emailed them. I got a reply from the man in charge and was told they weren't hiring yet. There were only three of them on staff, apparently, and he was shocked that I had even figured out their email addresses. Regardless, he kindly passed me on to the newly assigned news director, who told me the same thing—not hiring, but send me your CV. Which I did immediately.

After waiting a few weeks, I wrote again and asked if they were ready for applications. Still no, was the reply. So, I kept waiting. And emailing. Always respectful, sometimes funny. I wanted them to keep me in mind.

Amused by my determination, I was eventually invited to meet with the new bosses—just for the heck of it. I was told to not think of it as a job interview because they were not yet able to do that. Sure, I said, got it. I sent my CV again and prepared a showreel—which had quite a bit on it thanks to my friends at CNN who put it together for me. I was also going to Manila for Christmas the following week, so the meeting was a great send off. I was feeling good, and I had my sister and some cousins visiting from abroad.

As I loved to do, I was showing the visitors around London by taking them on my favourite adventure—walking along the river

Thames. We went west from Tower Bridge past Shakespeare's Globe, Tate Modern and the South Bank to cross over Hungerford Bridge and head towards Leicester Square and Covent Garden, where I was to leave them and go to work by Oxford Circus for the late shift.

Descending the steep rather uneven stairs from Hungerford Bridge, I slipped on a beer can—and no it was not mine. Thankfully, my cousin's hubby-to-be broke my fall. Not that he had a choice. He was in front of me, and I landed on him. Determined to make it to work, I insisted I was fine. So, I hobbled a few feet away to Embankment Station, deciding to take the tube to lessen the distance I had to walk. I was sure I could make it. But once I got to the train platform, it was evident there was no way I could go any further. I rang the office from a phone box, and my cousins put me in a taxi home …

…Where I had to climb three flights of stairs to get to the flat. With a foot that I still refused to accept may have been broken. Like a penitent in Manila's Baclaran Church, I got down on my knees and went up three floors like that. It was not easy. I was bruised by the time I got to the top. Somehow, I managed to ice my foot, and told myself I'd be fine in the morning.

The next morning, my foot was three times its normal size and blue. Like a smurf. So, my sister took me to A&E, which is what the Brits call their emergency room.

The foot was fractured. Doctor put me in a removable cast since I insisted on flying to Manila that weekend. This way, I would be able to adjust how tight the brace was. They also gave me crutches and advised me to stay off the foot as much as possible. Sure, yes. Thank you.

Well-meaning friends told me to cancel or postpone my meeting with Al Jazeera, which was supposed to happen the next day, but there was no way I was going to do that. These execs were kind enough to meet me even when they had yet to start the hiring process, so I wanted to get in there ahead of the game. Especially as I was going to be in Asia for quite some time on leave.

So, off I went the next day—managed to put on a suit, with my crutches and cast (it was quite a look). My sister came along with me for literal support. She held open doors, and had to help me climb stairs, get in taxis, and shuffle down hallways.

Soon as I walked into the meeting, which took place in a borrowed room overlooking Westminster Bridge (they still had no offices), the two executives' jaws dropped at seeing the state I was in.

'We could've postponed …'—*not a chance*, I replied before the guy in charge could finish. I wasn't going to miss this for the world. He laughed and said he was impressed by my 'determination'. I honestly hadn't set out to do that. I just really *really* wanted to meet them.

I handed them my showreel, and they went into a room to watch it as I waited. A few minutes later, one of the execs came out and told me to head in to see the guy in charge. She made her exit, saying nothing more than that. I was so glad to see him smiling when I walked in. He chuckled quite a bit over my 'gumption' and 'tenacity'. We talked about Baghdad, and that made me smile. At that point, I could talk about Iraq for hours, no matter how coloured in pain the memories. Some fifteen minutes later, the meeting was over. And it felt like I'd been sitting with an old friend. I was also no longer anxious about getting a job. A few months later—when they were ready—I was hired.

So that—and a crushed beer can—is how I went from one international network to another. London let me believe in myself and helped me trust my gut. Where determination led, fear and failure were not options. Yes, you can make sure there are safety nets to cushion a fall, but what I learnt is that if you don't weigh yourself down with anxiety or doubt, and **if** instead **you truly believe**—even with a broken foot—**leap and you will fly**.

EPILOGUE

AND NOW WHAT?

You know how when you're in grade school, at the impressionable age of like five or six, and you learnt everyone's full name in class? Then years later, that's still how you refer to them? Somehow, it stuck. First and last names, no nicknames. It's the same with several people I met through work. I mentioned a few of them in the Prologue and wanted to acknowledge them here. They burn in my memory like stars. Appearing like ever fixed marks that transcend geography.

Much of life is challenging, to say the least, and though I may intentionally choose to hold on to the positive, that does not erase the pain that exists. And I am forever marked by the anguish and the strength of the people below:

Lola Pilar Frias. One among hundreds of women forced into sexual slavery by the Imperial Japanese Army during World War II. We followed her pursuit of justice for years. I was humbled and left mute by her fortitude. How she survived in the face of such inhumanity. So many of these women lived with the trauma and their nightmares into their eighties, which is why they were each referred to as 'lola', Filipino for grandmother. The horror they experienced was unfathomable, but Lola Pilar recounted it. In song. Can you imagine an expressionless eighty-year-old woman, with a scar on her face from the sword of a Japanese soldier, stoically singing to you about being repeatedly raped? I will never forget it.

Mansura Abu Sha'ar. A Palestinian housewife born into a conflict she couldn't escape. She was seventy-three when we met her in Rafah, but looked a hundred, having lived in constant fear of death. The anxiety etched on her face has stayed with me. So has the way her body struggled to even move under the weight of her powerlessness. But through the interminable tremors of her dread, she raised a family.

The Miparanum Brothers. Both in their senior years, they were dominated by what they saw as the fatefulness of their situation. They lived in a conflict-ridden area where their father was killed, and they watched neighbours die. They maintained they had little other choice but to participate in the bloodletting. They had to get revenge and help those who needed the same. So, they became gun-makers for all sides of any conflict. The brothers could take any old metal and turn it into a weapon. And they lived out their days in the middle of a bustling town, in a ramshackle home under the shade of a beautiful, bountiful tree.

Rupert Macawili. Who had a soft if faraway smile on his face when I met him. He looked wistful, which made sense when you learnt he lost nearly fifty members of his family in a super typhoon. The worst, at the time, on record. His island looked like it had been stepped on by a rampaging mob of deities. Nothing but endless piles of debris. The sixty-three-year-old had been wandering around listless but offered his services as our driver. A week in—because he'd been mostly silent until then—he explained he wasn't doing it for the money but to survive. Money was pointless, he said, with things as they were, but he had to stay busy to keep from going mad.

Janice Joy Pampangan. Wasn't part of our original assignment. We were in a neighbouring province on another story when we heard that the body of a Filipino overseas worker had just been returned to her family. They were told she died from natural causes but believed she was killed by her employer. We heard she was so badly beaten she was almost unrecognizable. Stories like this were not in the news. Migrant workers coming back in body bags? We drove to her home and saw the remains. Emaciated and nearly black from all the bruises. One of her eyes had been beaten out of her face. While there, we learnt of another family in a nearby village who just received word that their daughter working overseas had suddenly died. The government said it would investigate, but they had to tread a thin line, needing to protect their citizens without alienating diplomatic partners. There was not much else officials could say. But the body bags and the silence of the families spoke volumes. Of forgotten martyrs to a cause they didn't choose. A battle they didn't create. Fighting to get out of poverty in a country whose riches were purloined by the corrupt.

Clarita Ala. Who lost four of her sons to the most popular president her country has had. A self-confessed murderer and rapist. Go figure. Everyone remembers him, but they don't remember her children, who didn't even get to be adults. Nor do they recall Clarita, who remained unheard though she'd been fighting against this man's 'way of governance' from the start.

'Jesse' and **'Boy'**. Hired hitmen in a brutal ambush that killed fifty-eight people. I sat with each of them as they spoke out against the powerful political clan who planned the massacre. Within a year, both the men were dead.

And then, there's **Norman Surplus.** A man from Northern Ireland who battled cancer and flew around the world in a gyrocopter in celebration of life. The journey in the small, open-air rotorcraft should have taken four months, but between international licensing challenges and mechanical issues, it took him nine years. Norman said he was helped by so many people along the way, and in most places, only encountered the best of humanity. He died of a heart attack while battling his third round of cancer, three years after accomplishing his goal. I will always remember his determination and infectious optimism—and how it felt to up in his aircraft. He flew me around for a little bit, after which I completely understood his enthusiasm. It was like my childhood dream of flight come true.

Guideposts

For me, life ebbs and flows like the rivers I've marked here. And along the way, there have been docks or ports that have offered shelter. I had guided my ship on the presence of my parents. So, when I lost them, I was literally lost at sea. A few years after losing my father, my mother died on the morning of Christmas Eve. About a month after that harrowing super typhoon.

Like Rupert, I returned to work to stay afloat. Which meant going back to the scene of the typhoon's devastation. I needed to be useful and do something meaningful. Only to find myself empathizing a little too much with a fourteen-year-old boy who had lost his mother in the storm. As he recounted his story, I couldn't help but weep. I was grieving for him … and for myself. That's when it began to dawn on me that I might need a break.

Days later, I took one. To clean out the home in which I was raised. For weeks, I sat amongst my parents' things—pouring over every piece of paper, every knickknack, every photo—reconstructing their lives. Trying to understand, bit by bit, what mattered. After all they'd lived through and shared—was this all there was? A houseful of dust and cobwebs, and knickknacks? It was a personal confrontation with mortality, and I began to ponder what it is we have to hold on to in the end.

And so, this book.

I had to learn to say goodbye to the family home and the roots that it gave me. And I unmoored my ship from the past to sail ahead. Bringing with me everything that mattered. The memories—some knickknacks—and the love. Guided as always by the stars.

When You Wish Upon a Star

Also in grade school, we learnt this Disney song about making wishes and faith granting your heart's desire no matter who you were. But as soon as we understood the lyrics, well-meaning adults taught us it wasn't true. That life was difficult, and often 'unfair'. That we were meant to struggle and suffer. That people would be unkind.

It's a good thing I—like a cat—am easily entranced by sparkling lights. As a child, this meant I was fascinated by the cosmic, technicolour stars in science fiction movies, and glued to TV shows about space travel and aliens. Which may explain the favourite childhood pastime mentioned in an earlier chapter: playing interplanetary travellers with imaginary spaceships and transporters.

Point is: I always preferred to look beyond what I was told was 'real' and tried to find something … more. Something less confined and a little more magical. That extra bit of special.

I guess, early on, something within told me there had to be more than what could be seen. Or touched. That reality itself could not possibly be limited to what we arrogantly thought we 'knew'. That we couldn't allow ourselves to be trapped and defeated by— or feel victim to and wallow in—sadness and despair because of life's injustices. So, yes—I believed in fairies … and angels …

and time machines … (and *Star Trek*) … and miracles. Funny then that a 'dreamer' like me (as I was often called) would end up working in journalism. Or maybe—serves me right?

In 2016, after nearly eleven years with Al Jazeera, I felt it was time to finally lay down my reporter's mic and pivot.

You would think that being confronted every day of the last two decades or so with natural calamities, war, poverty, disease, and every other conceivably ugly thing in this world would strip a *dreamer* of their faith in magic … but it hasn't. Quite the opposite is true. I have found that underneath all of life's pain and harshness, it is by pure magic that people survive.

So, in a nutshell, here's the crux of what I've learnt that I wanted to share: helped along by a series of serendipitous things flowing into each other, we're all connected and we'd see it if we stayed open.

Be present. And when an obstacle arises, trust your gut and pivot where needed. When that's difficult, respect where you're at and breathe. In that pause, in that *silence*, you can tap into a greater wisdom, which—surprise—resides everywhere and within. So, believe in the poetry of life—and soar.

We are all made of stardust …

thank goodness for that!

ACKNOWLEDGEMENTS

For their constant support, I would like to express eternal gratitude to my family. Particularly my siblings, Inés, Cristina, and Anton, with whom I have had the good fortune to share parents. All my love. And thank you.